Deer, Dragonfly, and Cardinal

the story of a boy and the mother
who is always looking for him

Jean Robison

Printed in the United States.

Cover and book design by Asya Blue Design.

ISBN 979-8-9921817-0-8 Paperback

ISBN 979-8-9921817-1-5 Ebook

For Andrew, Michaela, and Jim

CONTENTS

PROLOGUE

Two months after my twenty-four-year-old son left this life for the Other Side, I recognize a burning need to write his story. What has transpired over the past four years is a memoir borne of what it was like to raise Andrew and have a unique relationship with him as his mother and friend. I share the perfect baby I held in my arms, the curious, adventurous little boy I watched over with love and awe, the striving teenager who went after all his endeavors with grit, and the young man who fought like a warrior to keep going in the face of overwhelming obstacles. I also share the fullness of my grief: numbness, shock, feeling betrayed by the universe that everything will work out, enduring the pain of the anniversaries, the birthdays, all of the holidays, and the triggers around every corner. I am getting through it, even though I thought I could not, and I am taking care of myself, a process that grows stronger as I work on it.

Grieving the loss of Andrew asks me to hold two things at the same time: the truth of losing him, and his daily presence in my life. The discovery that his life continues on the Other Side is wondrous, loving, and surprising, even with my broken and bruised heart. Andrew actively makes connections with me in multiple ways, and this gives me a perspective of the grander scheme of the universe and slows me down from focusing only on regret and pain. They keep me hopeful and from becoming too bitter. Losing this beautiful boy is unbearable without having the strong, authentic spiritual bond with him that I gratefully experience.

To all emotional warriors who have lost a child or a loved one, I stand with you in solidarity. It is not an easy road. As my boy told me, don't look down, and keep your head up.

NOTES ON MY SPIRITUALITY

My spiritual side is broad and deep. Over decades of searching and seeking, I have cultivated a blend and balance of belief systems and practices that feels right for me. As a young child, I felt a level of safety and comfort with Jesus, Mary, going to Sunday school, singing in the youth choir at church, and referring to myself as a Protestant. In my college dorm at the University of Oregon, I met a girl from San Francisco who introduced me to the teachings of Ram Dass and Eastern religions, opening my eyes to other spiritual practices. Years later, I studied Hinduism and Buddhism as part of my yoga teacher training, and I found the practices and teachings resonate deeply with me, but I don't walk away from my childhood beliefs. One of my favorite mantras is "Lord Jesus Christ, have mercy on me," which kicks in when I am low.

The very day Andrew dies, I tell myself I will need to connect to my spirituality and deepen my practices more than ever. I seek healing to learn about myself, expand my beliefs, to be open to all possibilities, and to connect with

Andrew. I visit a psychic, receive hands-on Reiki, and have my Akashic Records (a blueprint or recording of each soul) read and explained to me by a certified practitioner. I learn the formal practice of TM (Transcendental Meditation) and meditate every day, cross-legged on a cushion in front of my Buddha surrounded by crystals, shells, and stones. Through the Unitarian Universalist minister who officiated at Andrew's funeral, I find a shamanic healer, a grounded, spiritual woman and mother, and she is key to helping Jim and me understand the Other Side and what Andrew may be experiencing in his new realm. She comes to our house to clear the energy, heal the trauma that took place, and to bless us and our home by accessing higher spirits and guides that come through, including Andrew himself.

While meditating, I often ask the question, "Andrew, are you with me?" and I hear an inner voice reply, "Mom, I'm always with you." Some days are easier than others, and on a tough day it is all I can do to stay put on the cushion as my thoughts race, but I go back the next day. The more I remain dedicated to the practice of meditation and seeking communication with him, the deeper I go and the more connected I feel to Andrew.

Whenever Andrew appears to me in a dream, I write down every detail, including his approximate age, his appearance, his clothing—all of it matters and provides deep meaning. Andrew's dreams and visitations are wonderful gifts that I reflect upon, learn from, and share.

My spirituality is a guidepost that I need so much in those early months, and as time moves on, it is a balm for panic attacks and spontaneous bouts of deep sadness. It enables me to take a leap into the unknown. My psychic gifts and intuition may come and go, but if I keep my channels open, they allow me to keep the faith, stay connected to Andrew, and travel my own spiritual journey.

Andrew came to earth with courage and purpose to undertake the Hero's Journey with all of its challenges, and he was excited about the adventures ahead of him. When the obstacles became too much for him to bear, he completed his time here and returned to Source, our origin, a place where the self can heal, spiritually.

I refer to Source and the Other Side interchangeably throughout this book as an acknowledgment that Andrew has moved beyond the earthly realm, and yet he is still very connected to me on this side. I believe that in his new realm, Andrew is free to be a soul with no boundaries nor harsh timelines as he ascends to becoming a spiritual master.

This book is my experience of Andrew's spirit in earthly and celestial forms. I refer to him in present tense throughout, as I know he is always with me.

PART I:

THE OTHER SIDE

*Reader discretion advised. "The Deer and the Detective" describes a suicide. If you are experiencing suicidal thoughts or a crisis, please reach out for professional help or call the suicide hotline at 988.

RUNNING IN HIKING BOOTS

Andrew is about twenty-one. I am up close to his face, a cameraperson viewing him in extreme closeup. He does not make eye contact with me as he ties his hiking boots. He is on one knee on a narrow plateau, a grassy strip of land nestled among clouds and fog on both sides, getting ready to run. In this dream, I am a disembodied soul, and Andrew has invited me to watch him.

When he finishes tying both boots, he stands up. He is wearing a Dri-FIT athletic shirt, baggy shorts, and high socks. He starts running slowly, and each step makes a BOOM sound on the ground beneath him. His alternating feet accelerate with a loud rhythmic pattern: boom . . . boom . . . boom . . . boom, boom, boom, BOOM! He passes me on his left and runs even harder until he reaches a cliff. I watch the back of his body as he jumps high into the ether, arms overhead, and then he lets go, falling into the mist with his arms still above him, until he is gone.

I wake up.

Andrew loves running as a middle and high schooler, but as an adult, anxiety and depression take over, and one day, running is over. Spirit Andrew, however, does whatever he wants on the Other Side; there are no obstacles. With hiking boots for his long journey ahead, he invites me to see that he can run now, and by jumping off the cliff, he lets go of his earthly life to dive into a solo adventure, free from the ties that bind him to earth, back to Source.

THE DEER AND THE DETECTIVE

A seasoned detective in all-blue pulls up to a home on a quiet street around 4:15 a.m. She is greeted by a young deer standing sentry to the left of the house. She gets out of her patrol car and faces him. He stands tall and looks her in the face. She talks to him, confirming, "It's you, isn't it, Andrew?" He continues to look at her, then he turns and scampers back into the woods behind the house. She walks quickly through the front door.

Jim awakes abruptly at 3:00 a.m. He tries everything to get back to sleep, but he is wide awake, completely unlike him. At 4:00 he notices a light is on downstairs, so he goes down to make sure Andrew is OK.

A primal, male scream rips me out of my sleep. I sit up and wonder if the scream is coming from Andrew or Jim. A moment later Jim runs into our bedroom; his body is frantic, jerky. Andrew must be gravely hurt, or worse. Jim is alternating between, "He's gone!" to sobbing, "He's cold, he's cold," his body curled up and rocking. I leap out of bed, dash through the hallway and the kitchen and stumble down the basement stairs, Jim one step behind. Just before reaching his bedroom, I note that the light to the laundry room is on, and my eyes go up to a teal green strap I have never seen before. My boy's face is angelic, almost in awe, but his eyes no longer see us. The image of one Adidas slip-on sandal still on his right foot and the other toppled over on the ground registers in my brain. He has flown away or been taken away by someone or something that is beyond us. I fall away from the scene in shock, my mind simultaneously thinking, *This is too big for the two of us* and *There must be some solution*—although I know there is not—so I quickly call out the only thing that comes to my mind: "Call 911, call 911, call 911." Jim makes the call. The police are there within minutes.

A young policewoman arrives first, along with several men who run downstairs, leaving Jim and me in the living room. She looks like she is in her early twenties. She has dark hair with big eyes and a grounded presence. She watches me closely, sitting by my side the whole time, helping me to the kitchen when I think I may have a little breakfast, picking me up with my husband when I collapse on the floor, then ushering me back to the couch. I look at her and ask, "Why?" She answers like one who has seen things, despite her youth: "Unfortunately, it happens." It is an oddly comforting thought. It takes away the stigma and doesn't attempt to explain such a complicated thing.

The front door opens. A professional, seasoned detective in her mid-fifties with long brown hair in a ponytail runs towards me, gets immediately down onto her knees, holds both my hands, and silently looks into my eyes with a knowing, deep sympathy. No words are spoken.

After some time and a short investigation, we somehow manage to explain Andrew's life, his autism, anxiety, and depression; his struggles, and our efforts to seek treatment, all within an hour of the detective's questioning. She tells us she has never seen any parents do more for their child than we did. This is nice, but I don't believe it. As she is leaving, I blurt out the question, "I loved him! Why wasn't that enough?!" She looks back at the two of us, middle-aged mom and dad in pajamas, bewildered and frightened on the couch, and says kindly and truthfully, "Because love is love, but love doesn't fix. If it did, we wouldn't be here right now." She then tells us that in her thirty years of doing this work, she always sees "Spirit finding a way to exit"—and this time, as she pulled up to our house, she was greeted by a young deer, who she knew to be Andrew.

She gives me her card, telling me to call her if I need her. I don't call her, but I never forget the gentle way this veteran detective treats us in this moment—with deep empathy, and respect. She holds us in a loving space and keeps us from moving towards a place of utter fear, danger, and chaos.

I may never see her again, but I am grateful she is the one that comes to us after the worst trauma of my life.

PART II

THE BOY

CELL PHONE CALL

Andrew is at scout camp, about eight years old, and he is running away from me. I see the back of his head with his blondish-brown hair, and I call out his name as I run after him, watching him disappear into the crowd. I push through hordes of boys and families, and the next thing I know I am chin-high in a public swimming pool, still calling his name. I ask people in the pool if they have seen him, but no one is paying attention to me—they are romantic couples having drinks and talking with one another.

In the next scene of the dream, I am on a bus that is taking me away from the camp, but I don't want to leave because I haven't caught up to him yet. I am his mother; I can't leave him behind. I stand up at the back of the bus and scream his name at the top of my lungs, "ANDREW!" I tell the bus driver to STOP the bus so I can get out. The bus driver doesn't want to, but I continue to scream so much that he lurches to a stop. I dash off the bus, take out my cell phone and dial Andrew's number. It occurs to me now that I am off the bus, neither one of us will be able to get home, but that is OK—I just want to find him, and then we will figure it out from there.

Standing there in the dark as the bus pulls away, the phone rings and rings, until I hear my own thoughts speaking to me: "There is no one on the other end to pick up."

I abruptly wake up.

I immediately realize the message of this dream: I cannot reach Andrew anymore through earthly means such as chasing him, yelling his name, or calling him on his cell phone. I struggle to process the harsh reality that my boy is gone, and I, his mother, can't get him back, ever.

This dream happens within the first week of his leaving us. The ending is matter-of-fact and delivers cold logic to a mother who thought she could solve everything with Andrew, if only she tried hard enough.

THE BOY

We talk, but we are not sure about having a second child. I am suffering from chronic sinus infections while working several part-time gigs as a dance instructor and choreographer, and Jim is putting in long, hard hours as an engineer. We are living in Bellevue, Washington, three thousand miles away from our families. No free babysitting. My daughter Michaela is an easy child to raise, and my ob-gyn tells me that if I want another child, I should do it soon: my right ovary was recently removed due to a dermoid cyst, and there is a chance of the same happening to my left ovary.

While up late one night with a bad cough, I reach my hands to the ceiling and plead to whomever is listening, "Should I have another baby?"

Immediately, my hands and arms start shaking, and I enter what feels like a spiraling tunnel that brings me into a darkened forest. I hear urgent whisperings into my ear, but I can't make out the words. I see the silhouetted profile of a baby, superimposed on the larger image of a toddler, cheek to cheek with me. We are both smiling widely, and his blue eyes stand out against his rosy cheeks, framed by sandy beach-blond hair.

The next morning, I write down the whole vision in detail in my journal and draw the profile of the silhouetted-baby. Three months later, I am pregnant. The ultrasound photo I receive matches the profile of my drawing.

The day I find out I am having a boy, I can't stop smiling.

I go into labor two weeks before my due date. The doctor confirms that although I am in labor, Andrew is not dropping into station, so I am given an epidural to relax the muscles. Two hours later, he is born. The mystery of his not dropping into station is revealed: the umbilical cord is wrapped around his neck, twice. He is a quiet, gorgeous baby, and APGAR scores are perfect.

Unlike his sister, who was colicky and screamed on and off for three months, Andrew is an easy baby. I bring him with me everywhere. Instead of putting him in the snuggly or the stroller when picking something up at Bellevue Square Mall, I carry him proudly in my arms or over my shoulder, and he looks around, never making a peep. A photography studio is having a special where a customer can get one free four-by-five photo of their baby right there on the spot, and I carefully hand over my precious one-month-old to the photographer who lays him gently on blankets and says he is the most beautiful baby she has ever seen.

Right before bedtime, Andrew often cries as if his heart is breaking. We turn off the lights in the living room, I put on an Enya CD, and Jim rests his baby boy on large, flat open hands and floats him, softly, gently, back and forth, back and forth until he drops off, then carries him into his crib to sleep soundly through the night.

As a toddler, he meets all the developmental milestones. Because he has a chatty, talkative older sister who constantly converses with him, he talks early with an advanced vocabulary, and he starts walking at the average age of thirteen months.

I start noticing a few small things, but nothing alarms me, yet. He looks around a lot and takes in the world around him, quietly, as if trying to figure it all out, rather than having a direct connection with the person he is with. One morning, when I go to pick him up in his crib, I watch and listen as he marvels at and whispers to the dust motes that are swirling in the sunlight through the window, smiling to himself rather than at me. He spends a lot of time alone playing with his toys, and he engages in cooperative play with other children his age. He is great with his hands and loves stacking blocks and manipulating objects. He starts having tantrums, but nothing too unusual, yet. He runs back and forth in our family room while humming to himself and flapping his hands, which we find adorable. He is so smart and so cute, and even if he sometimes has meltdowns and angry outbursts, we get through them. We go on lots of family vacations and adventures, and he always has a fun time.

In preschool, some of his teachers express concern about his not interacting with other children and for his inability to sit still. In kindergarten, his teacher tells us that he has a hard time staying focused on a lesson, and that he is often impulsive, such as throwing a felt letter across the room. By third grade, interactions with his teacher and classmates become more tense, and after his first official round of school testing, he is diagnosed with a "communication disorder." The process of receiving services in school a couple of times a week begins, such as lunch bunch, a pre-selected group of kids who all need help socializing, and one-on-one sessions with the occupational therapist and school psychiatrist. Although Andrew keeps it together most of the time at school, there are increasing angry, irrational outbursts at home that are alarming, such as screaming at his Aunt Julie to get out of our new minivan when she is inside admiring it, and a meltdown that goes on for hours when his sister goes to a friend's house. We reach out to mental health professionals for answers. We are told we are not addressing his aggressive behaviors with the right positive tactics as parents because he has ADHD, and we need to read books about it and change how we parent him.

When Andrew is finally diagnosed with high-functioning autism at age eight after a lengthy evaluation by a neuropsychiatrist and confirmed by a doctor, instead of it all coming together, I feel lost. Our family has a brand-new road map that doesn't make sense to me. I sob standing up in the lobby of the hospital as I think of the hard road ahead, beginning with no knowledge of this neurological challenge.

The years that follow the moment of the diagnosis contain steps that move him forward, miraculous moments that include joy and magic, but other steps move him back. He is bullied and isolated, endures name-calling and cyber-bullying.

He hides the worst from us because he thinks the bullies are the cool kids, and he can't risk offending them. It is incredibly painful to see how Andrew is motivated to fit in and yet finds himself increasingly alone in his hometown. Sometimes he makes a connection with a friend, but the problem is keeping friends as they drift away from him when they realize he is just too different. I am grateful there are some therapists and psychologists, in school and outside of it, who are caring, competent, and compassionate, committed to helping Andrew with his social challenges, but there are other professionals and educators who are not effective at all, and then we lose time and hope.

Some classroom teachers adore Andrew and praise his talents and his smarts; others are bewildered by having a child with autism in their classroom and have a hard time helping him to embrace and work with the diagnosis. His needs are real, and we feel alone and scared on this journey with too many twists, turns, and off-ramps that go nowhere; meanwhile, time is passing by, and with age, his path gets harder instead of easier. As friends fall away and the birthday invitations stop arriving in the mail, he is smart enough to recognize autism as something more than what we all bargained for.

When Andrew is in fifth grade, the night after a successful piano recital, he becomes extremely ill from what we learn later is the result of a tick bite at the back of his neck. Even though the tick is removed by his doctor, Andrew is not given an antibiotic; this is unfortunately during a period of time when our pediatrician is reluctant to treat tick bites if there are no immediate symptoms. A few days later, I come home from work to find him lying deep under his covers in the middle of the afternoon, completely lethargic, and this scares me more than anything. I scream to Jim that Andrew is very sick, and we need to get him to the closest hospital. We rush him to the ER, Jim carrying his small body into the lobby where we are greeted with a wheelchair. While being examined, I am terrified, and Andrew turns his face to me and says, "I knew you wouldn't let me die . . . because you love me."

He is diagnosed with cerebellar ataxia, an inner-ear disorder that affects his balance, resulting in fatigue, vertigo, and nausea. I break down and cry every time I am with him in the hospital room, terrified of losing him, while also being amazed at his bravery in enduring it all. He cannot stand, walk, or sit up to eat without getting dizzy and vomiting violently, often with blood. And yet this is also a sweet time as he lets me cuddle with him in his hospital bed and read books to him, which is one of my favorite memories of being his mom.

After one week, he is still sick and on an IV for fluids and nutrients, and when he is at his most exhausted state, I just want him to yell at me, to get angry, to rant about something—to do anything other than lying there, not moving. His fifth-grade teacher brings him posters, balloons, and hand-drawn cards from every child in the class, and when he reads them, he comments, "They just wrote that because she told them to." Showing no improvement after a week, it is agreed he should leave the suburban hospital where he is languishing and be moved to Children's Hospital in Boston. I ride in the ambulance with him at night as he clutches a teddy bear, eyes wide open even in the dark, looking around and taking in all the dials and equipment surrounding us. It is a quiet, peaceful ride.

He starts to slowly recover in his second week due to many eyes on him at Children's, including a top neurologist. He gets the strength to begin building a thousand-piece Star Destroyer Lego that his Aunt Becky brings him. This demanding kit gives him the will to get better. One day while sitting up and working on it, the nurse takes out his IV to see how he does on his own, but she later tells him he is still dehydrated and that it must go back in. He starts to protest, crying quietly, his hands holding his Lego pieces. I jump on the bed to hold him tight during the procedure, and the nurse tells me with annoyance that I am "not helping." I fight back by telling her that this boy is tough, that this boy *never* cries, and if he needs to cry right now, he should be allowed to. He quietly sobs as she slides the needle back into his small hand, and then he goes back to work on the Star Destroyer. A Jedi knight, through and through.

One evening, the nurse suggests that I try to give Andrew a bath. With his limited coordination and our using a tiny, triangular-shaped hospital tub, he slips and slides around as I try to wash his hair and his body, which have not been washed since he was admitted. At one point he unexpectedly urinates right into the air like a fountain, and we look at each other and burst out laughing. It is a shared human moment, and one that I look back on as one of many times when Andrew and I connected on a shared level of humor.

After getting well enough to sit and stand, Andrew relearns to walk, which doesn't take long. We hold hands as he lurches down the hospital hallways, making laps, both of us laughing and stumbling together all the way. After two weeks of hospitalization, Andrew recovers from what is determined to be ehrlichiosis, a dangerous tick-borne illness, and is well enough to come home and back to school, but it is a tough road of recovery with a few relapses until he is finally back to normal. His normal. Having autism.

Although the diagnosis of autism prescribes a tough life ahead for him, I do not want the label to completely define his childhood years. Throughout Andrew's life, he proves himself over and over to be a fighter, such as learning to walk again after cerebellar ataxia. He is a striver, a hard worker, a warrior, a musician, an athlete, and a hero. Although his life doesn't always go smoothly, and the dreams he plans for himself don't come through the way he hopes, he gives our family the gift of himself, every moment of every day.

While on this earth for twenty-four years, my boy shows us joy, passion, and grit. His life is a testament to the miracle he was on earth, and the miracle he continues to be in the world beyond.

THE JOY

Andrew's early days are joyful and joy-filled. His sister Michaela is his constant companion, and his life centers around them having as much fun together as they can while being wacky. They make up skits and play dress-up in her nightgowns, and she fashions him in supermodel attire. They find comrades in each other, and they are as funny, playful, and goofy as kids should be.

One of my favorite memories is of a two-year-old Andrew wearing a bright blue Thomas the Tank Engine costume for Halloween. He uses a wooden train whistle as he blows, "Toot!" and calls out, "Thank you!" after receiving a treat from each neighbor around the block. At age eight, Andrew joins a summer drama camp that he participates in for the next four years, and he throws himself into it full force, participating in improv games and shining in his first role as a grumpy hobbit in vest and pantaloons on a quest. He is a confident musical theater kid in *Schoolhouse Rock Live!*, belting out, "Unpack your Adjectives!" and in *Willy Wonka and the Chocolate Factory*, he sings "I've Got a Golden Ticket," with gusto in a tour de force solo performance as Charlie Bucket, zooming across the stage with abandon. I am rapt with joy when Grandpa Joe sings the iconic song, "Cheer up, Charlie," and I cry openly after the final lyric, sang beautifully while my little boy holds his head down, hiding a shy smile when he is reminded to "be glad you're you."

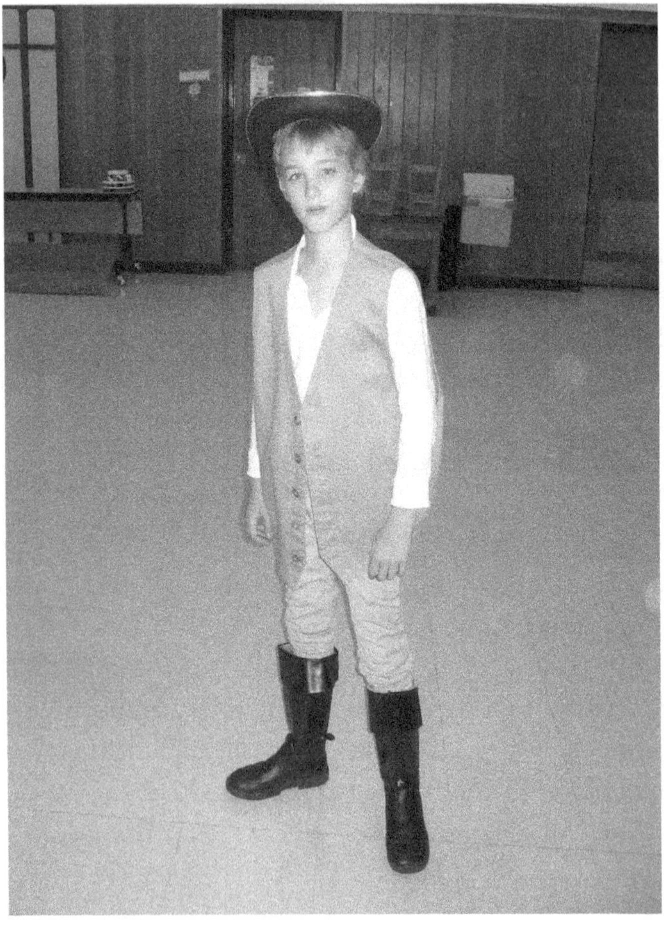

ALISON

When Andrew is eight years old, he announces he wants a puppy. I am not a fan of the idea. I never had a dog growing up—I am a cat person—and as a frazzled working mom, I don't like the idea of walking a dog every day and picking up their poop if Andrew turns out to be not up for the task. A perhaps larger reason is my being in graduate school at the time while working several gigs as a yoga, dance, and drama teacher, but when I explain all of this to Andrew, he throws his little body on the stairs and sobs into his folded arms, "Every little boy should have a dog." I make a deal with him: If he is a "very good boy," and does all the chores I ask him to do, he can earn five hundred points of good behavior and earn his dog. That would buy me some time; at least it will get me to summer when both kids are home from school and can take care of a puppy. Sure enough, for four months, Andrew takes out the garbage, clears the plates, unloads the dishwasher, and performs any other chore I can think of, and he easily racks up the points, faithfully tracked on a little white board in our dining room. He is done by June, just as I finish taking my final exams.

During his point-earning process, Jim and I research the best kind of dog for Andrew, and we decide a Labrador retriever will be the perfect fit. Andrew wants a dog that will play fetch, and we want a dog who will love him, no matter what. It is one of the happiest moments of my life when we find a roly-poly, affectionate yellow Lab puppy from a breeder in western Massachusetts, and I walk to the bus stop with her in my arms. When I meet Andrew on the sidewalk, I hand her to him without a word, and he scoops her up in his arms and buries his face into her warm body, snuggling her close.

Thus begins a beautiful friendship. He names her Alison after a girl he likes in his class. The name just fits her. He walks her every day and picks up her poop with never a complaint, and he does the even less fun job of picking up all the old, nasty poop in the backyard. He plays Chuckit with her and they run together in the meadow near our house. He curls up next to her on the floor, and they close their eyes together. He brushes her teeth every night, and if he is away for a weekend, he reminds us to brush her teeth, and we assure him, "Yes! Yes! We will!" (Although, much to my chagrin, we often forget.) I bring son and dog to an agility summer camp, and he teaches her skills that she learns quickly, such as walking across a high balance beam and moving through an obstacle course, and they earn an armful of ribbons, including my favorite: "Dog Who Looks Most Like His Owner." For "Dress-up Day with Your Sidekick," Andrew dresses like Batman and Alison is outfitted as Robin for a priceless photo.

Alison was in our lives for thirteen years. She was his constant friend to hug, cuddle, and be consoled by. Sadly, she was also very anxious when he was stressed, and she would curl in my lap and tremble if he was having a meltdown. She had cancer three times, followed by surgeries to remove each tumor, and she was miserable afterward as she bit the stitches or gnawed on the healing wound, which meant she had to wear a cone 24-7 to avoid injuring herself further.

The timing of putting her down was terrible: Andrew had left college after completing his junior year because he was isolated, depressed, and overwhelmed by the schoolwork, and staying was no longer an option for him. The veterinarian told us that Alison's cancer will return, and we are told to choose chemo, radiation, and/or amputation—all horrible choices. I thought the kind choice would be to let her go. But what was I thinking? Putting her down is the second hardest day of my life. I sob hysterically while Andrew and Jim kneel next to her, silent and completely shell-shocked by her passing.

I wonder how much her death affected Andrew. I comfort myself by thinking how their spirits are together now, a boy and his dog joyfully reunited and playing happily together again in the fields, both in the best of health.

INTREPID TRAVELER

Andrew never whines, "Are we there yet?" or cries because he is tired or hungry—he just has faith that we are off on an adventure, and he is going to enjoy it. We go to Paris when he is five years old, and he flies across the Atlantic on the red-eye, sleeping peacefully all the way. He is a trooper the whole time we are there, and this is one month after 9/11, and there are a lot of restrictions. At the entrance to Le Louvre, he obediently sticks out his little arms to the sides for his body to be scanned by the security guard, who is so taken by him that he tousles his hair and says something endearing in French. Andrew strolls through the long hallways, taking in the art with a seriousness of purpose. He rides public transit everywhere and walks miles through the city with a skip in his step and a smile on his face. He and his sister walk with their arms slung around each other's shoulders, an image I will later see in my dreams. He explores Jardin Luxembourg and other parks, fountains, and monuments, and he rides the Ferris wheel at Place de la Concorde, a ride that even I won't go on because it is frighteningly high. He climbs up the side stairs to the top of Notre Dame where the gargoyles look out over the city, the steep stairs of Montmartre, and many flights of stairs from the underground train to the sidewalk. He rides the merry-go-round near Tour Eiffel, and he reaches out his stick to loop the golden hoop. He eats trout at a restaurant, gobbling it up and giving the stink eye to the smokers in the restaurant, and at the end of a long day, he cuddles his tired body next to his dad on the Metro, eyes barely open, ready to head back to the hotel for a long, cozy sleep before the next day of adventures.

Andrew's first time at Disney World is also at age five—that was quite a year of travel for us! At rope drop, we all run to Tomorrowland to get our FastPasses for Space Mountain. While waiting, Andrew and Jim go on the Buzz Lightyear ride as buddies fighting the evil Emperor Zurg, and after it is over, Andrew steps out in a happy daze, looks around at the futuristic setting and small jets circling overheard, and says, "*Why* is this place so amazing?" When Andrew goes on Space Mountain, with Michaela sitting behind him, Jim and I are terrified—what are we doing, putting our precious little boy on this terrifying ride? He's so tiny! What if he falls off? When the ride is over, he jumps out like young Luke Skywalker, confident, unafraid, and ready for the next adventure.

NOTICED IN A CROWD

During a dance exhibition in Morocco at Epcot, several male dancers construct a wide, fan-like, human pyramid, and they look into the audience for a volunteer. Maybe it is Andrew's bright outfit—red tank top and patterned red shorts, which matches the all-red costumes of the Moroccan dancers—that gets him plucked from the crowd and hoisted up into the air, a sweet smile on his face without a single worry that these strangers have attached him to themselves, his darling body dangling off the ground.

Oh, yes, he gets noticed! When he is two years old, he is photographed *twice* during the same event, the Marblehead Festival of the Arts, a large-scale July 4 celebration held in Marblehead, Massachusetts. On a large open field filled with kids' activities, a photographer takes a four-by-five color photo of Andrew standing on one leg, paintbrush in hand, thoughtfully adding strokes of color to a mural on a sheet. This photo is later published on the first page of The Marblehead Times, and it is only after his death do I bring it to a framing shop to preserve this precious newspaper clipping. He is looking at the canvas with a seriousness of purpose, not at the camera nor at us. Maybe that's why it is the only picture of him that we can bear to have on our wall right now.

The second time he is photographed at this event results in him being the focal point in a full-page spread, hardcover coffee-table book, simply entitled *Marblehead*. Andrew is sitting in a sand-castle-contest racing car, completely absorbed, while the rest of our family is strewn about: my mother and father ankle-deep in the ocean talking to my brother-in-law while my sisters and I sit side by side, the backs of our heads and bathing suits visible to the viewer. Right smack in the middle of this photographic composition is a little blond boy who is enjoying a moment to himself in a sandy beach car.

This is the story of Andrew, a boy with so many gifts. As he grows up, his smarts, talents, and cuteness continue to be noticed and recognized. But more importantly than all of that, he is always uniquely just himself.

I am surviving the loss.

TRUE GRIT

More than anyone I know, Andrew has grit. It is tough for him—and my daughter, too—growing up in a competitive suburban New England town. It puts a lot of pressure on Andrew when he sees how much work he will need to do to keep up with his peers, but he does, because he has drive and courage. As angry as it makes me to look back and see how tough this town was on him, a better focus is to focus on the wins. Despite the heartbreaks, there is plenty to celebrate in looking back on Andrew's determination to succeed on his own terms.

SPORTS IN THE SUBURBS

Andrew loves drawing, Legos, reading, and having free time to do as he pleases. His first foray into soccer results in him sitting on my lap during practices, and he doesn't have the same competitive edge for T-ball that the other preschoolers have for whacking the Wiffle ball off the tee and running the bases. However, he figures out in elementary school that participating in sports is the only way he is going to survive on this suburban stage, so he becomes super-motivated to do all that he can to catch up.

At age seven, he joins Little League and becomes motivated to play catch and practice batting with his dad, every night and weekend. During games, it is tough watching him strike out, but it doesn't stop him from going back and practicing, and lo and behold, on a summer day's afternoon, Andrew cracks it long and hard and makes it to first base while Jim and I look at each other with mouths wide open in stunned joy.

Being an outfielder is not enough for this gritty kid; he insists on being a pitcher, so he and Jim work for hours pitching balls over the plate, until the coach finally puts him in. I think once or twice Andrew strikes someone out, but honestly, the most I hope for is watching him pitch it well enough for the batters to hit the ball. As the years go on, the sport gets more daunting as the pitches get faster and faster, and the poor guy gets his thumb broken the one time the coach tells him to bunt instead of swing. After that, he drops baseball, but I am glad he has the experience. He sure looks adorable in his baseball uniform with his fighting stance and bat over his shoulder.

He is fairly young when he becomes interested in basketball, and he participates in summer camp intensives with other young kids his age in a hot, sweaty gym in a nearby high school. It is fun watching him hustle up and down the court, sweating, like everyone else, but the kids won't pass him the ball, even when he is wide open and calls for it. At the end of the session, he doesn't receive a single award, unlike every other participant; even the fluffy awards, such as "hardest working," "most improved," or "best team player" go to every other kid except him. I am in disbelief—what happened to everyone getting an award for participation? —but for his sake I don't say a word. It is clear to my mother-tiger-self that he is marginalized due to his disability, and the coaches' attitude is to just ignore him completely. His only "award" is a chocolate bar that he picks off the floor when the coaches throw a bunch of candy all around the gym, announcing, "First come, first serve," or in my mind, here's your dirty-floor candy! While the kids dash around manically, scooping up as much candy as they can, not caring if there is enough for everybody, Andrew runs to one specific chocolate bar, picks it up, and smiles at it as if he is Charlie Bucket finding the golden ticket. We go home from basketball camp while I burn up inside but keep it together for him as he smiles and holds his single candy bar. Dignity and grit.

I am thrilled that during a middle school game with an afterschool team, Andrew sails the basketball all the way from the far side of the gym and *whoosh!* It goes in! For the second time of our lives as parents in the stands, we are ecstatic! He never makes another hoop again in a game, but it doesn't matter. He proves to himself he can do it, and my pride in that one *whoosh* stays with me all my life.

Even tougher is Andrew's determination to play soccer in high school without ever playing it before. I've never wanted to be a soccer mom, but once he realizes he wants to play, there is no talking him out of it. To make the odds of success even more daunting, I can't convince him to attend a summer soccer camp or clinic to play with other kids, acquire skills, and actually try to catch up. I think he knows his skills are far below grade level and therefore he will be grouped with younger kids, or he will be completely intimidated by the highly skilled soccer players his age, so he continues to practice on his own, dribbling and kicking the ball into the goal and running up and down the practice fields every weekend with his dad. He watches DVDs that his dad orders on how to play soccer. It is frustrating to me, but he is stubborn, and this is the best we can do.

For tryouts in his freshman year of high school, he keeps up with his classmates with the strenuous physical drills, and he makes the team because there are no cuts. Even on a no-cut team, however, he spends most of the season sitting on the bench, only allowed to play once at the very end of a game when it looks like the outcome will be a win no matter what. But he never complains; he is grateful to be on the team.

For the upcoming sophomore year, he practices again all summer—still refusing to go to a soccer intensive to train. With his dad, he dribbles and shoots the ball into the net, over and over. A week before school, he endures a grueling five-day tryout, where I catch glimpses of him running and doing endless drills in the boiling hot sun. On the last day of tryouts, I sit in the minivan, praying the outcome will go his way, but when I see him walking toward the car with his head lower than I have ever seen, I think to myself *the news is not good*. He tells me that he, along with five or six others, have been cut from the JV team. He says the other boys were crying. He does not cry, although I have to force myself, for his sake, not to cry for him. I never saw a grittier boy than in that moment.

BOY SCOUTS

Andrew is a super-gritty guy when it comes to Scouts. He attends every Tuesday-night meeting looking dapper in his uniform, and he signs up for almost every single trip: canoeing, hiking, and white river rafting, to name a few. He braves four Klondike Derbies where the boys camp inside tiny tents, three Scouts side-by-side for warmth in the deep woods at the coldest time of the year. As summer approaches, he tells me he wants to get certified in water safety so he can swim in the deep water, and after a week of private lessons, he passes the advanced test. Each summer for seven years, he packs up his big trunk for two weeks at Camp Squanto in Plymouth, Massachusetts, where he will play Magic Card games with fellow Scouts, participate in skits and relays, and get soaking wet with boat battles at the lake.

After the funeral, Andrew's Scoutmaster hands us a thumb drive chock-full of pictures of Andrew participating in all his scouting activities over the years, laughing, smiling, surrounded by troop members. Knowing he had pockets of happiness combined with purpose and grit on these trips makes my heart feel a sense of awe that there *were* good times, even if I didn't personally see all of them, while he was a Boy Scout.

Andrew earns a total of twenty-eight merit badges, which moves him to being eligible for earning his Eagle Scout. Andrew's choice for his Eagle Scout Project is the grittiest choice I could imagine. He is first offered painting picnic benches, which I was in favor of, but no, that would be too easy. He settles on building erosion bars in Noanet Woods in Dover. The prep for this involves excavating huge boulders with a pick and an axe before laying down two-by-fours across the trail so drainage can sluice excess water off. He does this hard, back-breaking work for hours, along with his dad, the two standard bearers, and a handful of scouts who come to help on certain days. There are many grueling work sessions that result in father and son putting on their headlights, packing up hoes, axes, and other sharp pointed objects into wheelbarrows in the complete black of night, and wheel it all out of the dark woods back to the car. Andrew never complains about having the hardest of all Eagle Projects of his troop.

The day he earns his rank of Eagle Scout at his Board of Review and is formally honored at the Court of Honor with letters from dignitaries, visits from local politicians, and the official Eagle Court of Honor cake, makes me feel like the luckiest mother of a son in the entire world.

SCHOOL

Andrew's attitude toward learning and education is based on his natural curiosity about the world. His academic subjects come easily to him. He asks lots of questions, and he is genuinely interested in many high-level, in-depth topics. After his elementary school class reads *Tom Sawyer,* he immediately reads its sequel, *Huckleberry Finn,* followed by the whole *Harry Potter* series, *The Lord of the Rings* series, the 007 series, and when he is older, *Dante's Inferno* and *Dracula.* He develops a unique, witty writing style, and his imaginative, unique drawing styles range from realism to surrealist Paul Klee.

Andrew always finishes his homework on time, even if it means doing so in the doctor's office so he can get it done and have free time later. When he is hospitalized as a freshman in high school for an in-patient psychiatric evaluation that lasts two weeks, he completes all the work assigned to him daily. His violin is with him, too, and he practices in a private room every day.

Andrew's smarts and talents are acknowledged at his high school with his induction into the National Honor Society, as well as the National French Honor Society, formal ceremonies that take place on separate evenings, celebrated by his mom and dad. Although so proud I could burst, after the award ceremonies I feel sad while eating desserts in the cafeteria because not one classmate comes up to him to say hi or to share congratulations. He is a miracle in our eyes, but his journey continues to feel lonely.

Perhaps Andrew knows he won't be here on this earth that long, and so he makes the most of what his life has to offer while he is here, like Saint-Exupéry's *The Little Prince*, a beloved family book that Jim read to our kids. As his proud mama, I will never forget him making it to first base, making that impossible shot on the basketball court, determination to stick with soccer, earning his Eagle Scout, and achieving impressive academic awards. My mother often says to me, "Andrew had so much courage." Yes, he did, and despite heartbreaks and isolation from peers, this little prince shows us his true grit.

LOVE OF MUSIC

Andrew possesses a gift for music that is expansive, playing piano, cello, and violin, and experimenting with genres that include classical, folk, indie, jazz, and classic rock from the 70's and 80's. Part of his fascination with music may have come from Grandma Emily, who plays the cello, Uncle David, who plays the piano, and Great-Uncle Quincy who plays the violin, and Andrew is indeed interested in following his family's legacy. I think another, deeper part of his love of music is having a place to express himself and what he is feeling. He is deeply personal about all of his musical choices. Jim and I always listen carefully when he plays one of his favorite tunes out loud in the car rather than with his earbuds, as it gives us a close look into his psyche.

Music is a nonverbal, honest, and safe communication from him to us. I am grateful he shares himself with us in this way while on earth, and from the Other Side.

PIANO AND SYNTHESIZER

Like everything else in his life, Andrew approaches his musical education with a passion. At age five, he begins taking piano lessons, practicing with a frenzied commitment and giving yearly recitals, just like his sister. He learns the basics of reading music easily, and before I know it, "Martha, My Dear" by the Beatles is pounded out many times a day by a little guy whose feet don't touch the ground. He perfectly executes the jazzy slides of "Cantina Band" from "Star Wars," and at Christmas time, he brings out the "Charlie Brown Christmas" song book, and the nostalgic, melancholy songs from the soundtrack ring throughout our small Colonial home.

As a hip-looking teenager with a rapidly growing collection of CDs, Andrew finds his strong rock and roll side. Unlike life in the '70s when my brother put together basement bands with his talented friends while I watched them jam in the basement, I need to sign Andrew up for afterschool School-of-Rock-style programs where instructors put a band together for your musical kid. It is less than ideal because rehearsals are only once a week, and even though Andrew is there every week to play the synthesizer, the attendance level of other band members is less than optimal. They never feel like a "real" band, but Andrew takes it seriously as he finds his place behind the keys. Eight weeks of rehearsals culminate in a final performance, and I love seeing him up there on stage with his rock-star-handsome synth player vibe in dark band T-shirt, faded blue jeans, black Converse, and shoulder-length blond hair. He looks and sounds the part, but I always want them to feature him more with vocal and keyboard solos. Can they not see how special he is?

ORCHESTRA

When Andrew is a toddler, he watches my mother play the cello at my sister's wedding, and somehow that sticks: he, too, wants to play the cello. Starting with elementary school, he plays the cello all the way through middle school in the orchestra and in a string quartet. He holds his own among his peers—not first stand, but not last, either. He takes lessons in town, but alas, he starts losing interest in the cello as he somehow gets it into his head that violin players are cooler, due to, in his mind, being a more challenging instrument, and he wants to give up the cello and make the switch. There is a boy in orchestra who sort of befriends Andrew, and because he takes violin seriously, it impacts my determined son. I try my best to get him to stick with cello because he would be starting violin from scratch, but he wants to pursue it and refuses to budge.

We drive to the big music store a few towns over where families rent instruments for their kids. We return the cello, but this time we buy the violin from a persuasive salesperson. I also need to find him a private teacher right away, as his orchestra teacher makes it clear that Andrew will need to catch up, and the transition is tough at first. But true to his grit and personality, he practices and practices, squeaking away, until he astonishes me by outchairing the boy that inspired him to take up the instrument. The boy made sure that never happened again.

Michaela has the violin; it is hers now. Maybe one day she will make music with it, or perhaps it will end up in the hands of another budding child musician who wants to take it up.

JAZZ BAND

Jazz Band is a small, elite power group that high school musicians audition to be a part of. Andrew is given an extremely difficult jazz piano piece, which he practices every day for an entire summer. He has a jazz piano teacher who works hard with him on that one piece while I walk Alison around the teacher's neighborhood. Before the summer is through, Andrew has played that song hundreds of times, and when he auditions with it for the band director, thank the heavens above, he is in.

Now Andrew has *several* hard pieces to practice but with the added expectation to be an improv musician, which he doesn't seem to pick up on his own. Can improv be taught? *Is* it being taught? Jazz Band seems designed for kids born with jazz in their blood, and I am not sure the music teacher does much to mentor or help a newbie figure this part out. When concert time comes, Andrew looks fantastic on the big high school stage with his black suit, pure white button-down shirt, and slender black tie. But he doesn't play as much as I thought because there is another pianist in Jazz Band, and they share playing time.

Andrew is proud of being part of this elite group, but while the other student musicians riff and blast solos as if they have been improv-ing all their lives, Andrew is hesitant when it is his turn. Even though their improv solos are big and brassy, Andrew's are short, sweet, and thoughtfully made, while I hold my breath. I can't deny the thrill I feel seeing my baby boy walk out on stage, sit on the piano bench, rest his long fingers lightly on the keys, and wait for the conductor to raise his baton, but it is a stressful experience for me as I wonder if it will be short-lived.

We no longer have the grand piano in our home, having returned it to its owner, my brother. The synthesizer stays in our basement with the rest of his life items. We are not sure at all what to do with it, and so it stays zipped up in its case, on its side, until we figure it out.

REACHING OUT

During a family session, a compassionate therapist asks Andrew to play a song for us from his playlist. Without saying a word, Andrew scrolls through his playlist and plays, “I am a Rock” by Simon and Garfunkel. He looks down at the carpet, the therapist is silent, and Jim and I are so struck with grief for his pain and loneliness that we can only let the tears stream down our faces as we hear the lyrics of the song that are so connected to our son.

One day in the car, Andrew asks me to play, “Naked as We Came” by Iron and Wine. I know the lyrics well, but I don’t realize that he that he, too, is aware of them, lines that instruct a loved one not to bury them if they die before them, but to spread the ashes outside. When “Orange Sky” by Alexi Murdoch comes on Pandora, Andrew says, “Leave it on.” When I listen to those lyrics now, it brings up an image of a young man seeing his family members standing near to him in a dream and finding redemption with their love. Reviewing lyrics to both songs, I see how Andrew uses music to prepare me for his departure at some point in the future.

A few months after the worst day of our life, Jim is outside at night, taking down the Christmas lights, when he suddenly bursts through the door and races to the iPad stationed on the kitchen counter. As he does, he quickly tells me that the song "Hitch a Ride" by Boston keeps playing over and over in his head, and he thinks that Andrew wants him to listen to it. I have never heard the song before, so Jim quickly pulls it up. We listen to it together as we read the lyrics by Tom Scholz. I cling to Jim, crying in joy and pain, as I understand this is a healing song as Andrew shares with us insight about how he feels about the decision he made.

We further read that Brad Delp, the gifted, iconic singer of the song, took his own life by suicide on March 8, 2007. Andrew's birthday is March 8.

I think about Tom Scholz and Brad Delp's collaboration on a song that is very poignant. This song allows me to connect to Andrew's feelings about leaving us in a tender way. It is beautiful and gut-wrenching how Andrew shares with us the language of music to speak for him, both on the earthly realm, and from the Other Side.

IT'S MAGIC

Michaela and I walk around Old Town in Alexandria, Virginia, looking for an ice cream shop on a sunny, April day in 2021, nine months after my daughter lost her brother. After a bike ride in the morning, we take a long afternoon walk among charming buildings and homes settled close to the brick-stone, steep streets. Going out to get ice cream is what I have always done with my kids, and it is one of my favorite motherhood duties. Our final decision is Ben and Jerry's rather than one of the trendy or touristy shops—it fits the mood, and you can't beat the flavors.

We walk into the bright shop with its big space for customers to wander around, and I peer at the choices through the slanted glass. I order a double cone with two flavors—mocha chip, my standard, and Americone Dream, a family favorite. As my cone is handed to me, the song, "It's Magic" by The Cars comes on the shop's radio. From the very first guitar riffs of the song, I feel Andrew here with us in this moment, using the song as a sign. I pronounce to the shop, "Andrew's here!" and start singing and dancing to the song. Michaela doesn't agree nor argue as she gets her cone while I spin and rock out around the mostly empty shop, except for a few ladies deciding on their choices.

Although Andrew loves The Cars, this song is not the first one to come to mind when considering his favorites. "It's Magic" is upbeat, pop, top-fortyish. He tends to listen to their punkier, edgier, and dark rocker songs. But I just *know* that Andrew is with us *now,* and the energy and joy of the song follows me out into the streets, where we find a bench to sit and lick our delicious ice cream while looking out over the bay, enjoying a perfect April afternoon.

Five months later, in mid-August, I do the thing I never think I have the guts to do: I go on Andrew's Facebook page. I don't even go on Facebook much myself anymore, if I can help it. I am depressed enough. Jim tells me that going on Andrew's page is rough, and yet here I am, home alone, doing the very thing I should not. This is likely to be the most triggering thing I can do.

But sometimes we do things we should not.

I watch an old video of Andrew singing and playing "Don't Fear the Reaper" on his keyboard while he is at college. He has a soft, earnest voice—and I love hearing him sing. I have seen this video before, as it is a few years old, but now it hurts in a whole new way. After fifteen minutes of emotional anguish, I say to myself, *You need to log off.* I know this is not a wise decision for my grieving heart, especially without Jim home to hold me if I have a meltdown.

Right before I log off, I make a decision to see what Andrew's very last post is. And there it is: a month to the day before he died, the YouTube video of The Cars singing, "It's Magic." The lead singer, Ric Ocasek, stares into the camera as he sings and walks on the water of a swimming pool in front of an admiring crowd of fans.

I am not sure of the symbolism of the video—is Andrew anticipating becoming Christlike and having the ability to walk on water? But feeling magic when I am with Andrew is something that I want to feel every single day.

PART III

WISDOM AND COMPASSION

ANDREW'S WISDOM AND COMPASSION

Andrew possesses a deep wisdom that he shares with me at key moments in my life. This wisdom comes in small, quiet bursts: a few words, a phrase, a short sentence, a response to a question, or even a small action such as walking away from me when things are tense, giving us both some time and space. These small moments in our relationship make me think deeper and save the day.

The following stories embody not just his wisdom, but the compassion of Andrew, who perhaps without knowing it, saves me from myself many times.

FISH AND CHIPS AND A BEER

I am waiting in a long line at a takeaway counter in front of a pub in England at Epcot Center while Andrew stands stiffly behind me. He fidgets—I feel his tension. He has autism, and together we are a middle-aged mother and a middle-school-aged teenage son; an unlikely pair at Disney World theme parks, I notice. It is his second time, but he remembers nothing of it when he was here as a toddler, when we were a fun family of four. Andrew and Michaela are in Colorado with Uncle Gene, while Andrew wants to do Disney again. It is a much quieter, subdued vacation with just the two of us.

I hold tightly onto two Styrofoam containers and a tall, red plastic cup of beer topped with white frothy foam. I dodge tourists and pass shops pushing British memorabilia and tea, my son close on my heels—my shadow. The benches in a miniaturized version of a London park are filled, so I plop down on a street curb and set up my food on my right, cup of beer on my left, facing the stage for an upcoming performance by "The Beatles." Andrew, however, does not sit beside me: he stands tall and straight as a stalk of corn, turning his head quickly right and left, scanning the crowd, suspicious. Even as I know this is not a good sign, I note his handsome profile, the angles of his New England-pale face, his thatch of sandy brown, blond-streaked hair. "Everyone here is old!" he says, disgusted with the legions of baby boomers filling the park, not a teenager in sight. I shrug as I tear off a generous piece of golden fried fish and pop it in my mouth. The greasy coating dissolves, and I chew the delicate white flesh while he looks down on me with a cross expression. I hand him his Styrofoam container and tell him to come back when the show is over, and off he goes with his supply of fish and chips, to where I know not.

The familiar sounds and upbeat lyrics of early Beatles fill the park as the sky darkens. I rock side to side to the familiar chords and lyrics while dipping slabs of cod in tartar sauce and french fries in ketchup. I stuff them in my mouth with greasy fingers, I gulp big swallows of cold, pale beer, and I am happy. Free. For the next fifteen minutes, I sing loudly to "Eight Days a Week" with food in my mouth interspersed with tipping the cup of beer to my lips. I'm free from scornful looks from a boy who cannot share my joy, free from, "Can we go now, *please*?"

When the applause dies down, I stand up, turn around, and there he is: his lean, quick body and serious face snaking through a horde of exiting tourists to meet up with me now that the concert is over. It is only then that I realize that his leaving me in England for twenty minutes is his gift to me. I ask him where he went, and he points down the way: he was sitting on a bench next to the lake and eating his fish and chips in peace. Just like I did. He wisely knew we both needed our own space to eat in the way we wanted to.

I throw away the container and the cup, and we proceed to France.

DON'T LOOK DOWN

During our mother-son visit to Animal Kingdom at Disney World, I find that I must be brave for his sake, something I am not used to. He used to be the fearless one, zooming down double black diamond ski slopes as a child, but he is much more cautious as he gets older. *Now I need to be his role model,* I think to myself as we watch the Expedition Everest rollercoaster from outside its fence. Andrew is hesitant to go on this epic ride, but at the same time, he really wants to. We watch its conclusion a dozen times as screaming riders plunge almost straight down from a dizzying height into a thunderous splash of water, and then we walk away to go on a less scary ride, to consider Everest at a later time.

After a frightening ride involving vicious, big-mouthed dinosaurs popping out, threatening and screeching in our faces, I am a nervous wreck, but it appears Andrew is ready now, so we get our FastPass tickets for Everest. Before we know it, we are being buckled in by an attendant. Andrew turns to me and says, "I changed my mind. I want to get off," just as the cart takes off at an alarming, no-way-off-now pace. Too late.

The first part of the ride involves a slow *click-click-click* of the cart as it climbs at a nearly forty-five-degree angle with nothing on either side, just sheer drop-offs. I feel panic overtake me, and I say, "Andrew, I'm scared." While he looks straight ahead, he says in a calm, wise voice, "Don't look down." At the instant he says this to me, my mindset changes. I stop looking down, and I look ahead as we continue to *click-click* our way to the top.

The ride is filled with mind-blowing twists and turns as well as an abominable snowman who pops up time to time, and at one point, it appears as if we are all going to be ejected into the sky above. I say to Andrew, "I'm scared," and he calmly responds, "It's almost over. We are going backwards, and then we're going down the waterfall." I relax into it, and he is right. He memorized the sequence of the ride, having watched it so many times. I look on this experience and think about how he saves me with the words, "Don't look down" and "It's almost over." I think they are some of the most tender, loving words he has ever said to me.

This moment connects to a very compassionate moment between mother and son, a few years after this trip. I am going through a tough time at work. I am not recognized and underappreciated for my hard work, and it is taking a serious toll on my self-esteem. One day, I share the situation with Andrew. He thinks about it for a minute and says, "Mom . . . hold your head up." And it keeps me going. Every day I go to work for the rest of that year, I hold my head up, and I think of Andrew as the wise being who has my back. Don't look down. Hold your head up.

THE RIGHT RESTAURANT

Whenever we travel together, Andrew wisely chooses the right restaurant. Not only is the food perfect, but the atmosphere fits the mood, whatever the mood may be at the time.

This becomes very apparent during our second mother-son trip, to Washington state when he is 23. Andrew was born in Bellevue, Washington, a thriving suburb of Seattle, but we left when he was two, and he remembers very little of it. He wants to see his roots, and I have friends and family in the area, so off we go together. I am hoping this will give him a lift, as he is showing signs of serious depression. I think he is hoping this will give him clarity and purpose about his life.

When we first arrive at SeaTac Airport, I can see wonder in his eyes. The sad, tense look is gone as he peers out the window of our rental car at the tall trees and the Seattle skyline. Our first stop is the Bellevue Botanical Garden, a place I loved when we lived in the area for eight years. We meander around paths and take photos of each other in the serene setting of a Japanese garden and soothing water features. For lunch, Andrew agrees to the museum's café. We order fresh veggie sandwiches and eat outside at a table on the hillside with a view and the sun on our faces. I text Jim to tell him he loves it here.

From that point on, for every upcoming meal, Andrew hunches over his phone to research the best place to eat. In every case, he nails it: a small, under-the-radar Italian restaurant in trendy Kirkland where we eat delicate, homestyle seafood dishes for dinner, and the next day, for lunch, a tiny Greek café in Issaquah that serves authentic chicken kebobs with rice and vegetables. In both cases, our meals are served by gentle waitstaff, and not only is the food delicious, but the atmosphere in each restaurant is also calming, an essential quality for Andrew and for me.

Andrew also knows not to pass up a good thing. When we go to the town of Snoqualmie Falls with my friend Karen, we tell him to choose between a small, relaxed taco café or the famous diner used in the '90s TV series, "Twin Peaks." He goes back and forth, but he finally chooses the diner, and he is happy to be surrounded by all the memorabilia from the show on its walls while he calmly eats a comforting, home-cooked diner-style meal.

The one disastrous restaurant is my fault. I choose an over-the-top, glitzy place in downtown Seattle where we sit outside on a small balcony overlooking a dock filled with boats and yachts and a full view of downtown with its iconic Space Needle. I'm happy to be next to Puget Sound, eating and sunning by the water at the same restaurant I visited in my thirties for special occasions, but Andrew is antsy sitting outside, and he becomes angry when a helicopter zooms overhead. This is one of his most severe phobias, thinking that helicopters are stalking him. He says, loudly, "We need to go inside, now!" and we finish our lunch quickly in the dark cavern of the restaurant. The rest of the day is tense and lonely as he stops speaking to me. I drive us up north just to sit on the shoreline in Bothell, lying on a towel on a cool, breezy day on a small strip of a sandy beach while he paces back and forth nearby, ferries gliding in and out as a silent hour goes by. All I can do is lie there and decompress, and all he can do is walk back and forth, both of us in our very alone states of mind.

One night, we get into an argument in the middle of downtown Bellevue about where to eat. Nothing seems to work until he finally mutters, "Let's just go to Panera." I park in the lot, and he immediately opens the door, slams it, and goes inside to order. I take a few moments to compose myself and then calmly walk in to order a simple dinner of soup and salad. Once again, he wisely knows this is the perfect restaurant for us to decompress in our own space as we sit at separate tables, having a chance to breathe and eat.

One of our final meals in Bellevue is at a very busy, somewhat high-end Italian restaurant with absolutely delicious food. Andrew has approved of the menu and the place in advance, and while my friend Karen and I enjoy our meals and conversation, he eats up every single bit of his dinner quickly and then allows us to take our time catching up while he explores the hotel. These are the times I just let him go, trusting that he will come back as he always does.

After dinner, we go for a leisurely walk around the large fountain at Bellevue's downtown park. I tried a few days earlier to walk around the spacious park with Andrew, but he was too anxious, so I strolled by myself while he paced near a park bench until I returned. This time is different because he feels comfortable around Karen. After a fun day visiting the beautiful Snoqualmie Falls waterfalls, he now leads the way, and the three of us walk the complete circumference of the park with its long, low, man-made waterfall and wide, open space. I take a picture of him from behind; he is wearing his faded blue Old Navy hoodie, cargo shorts, and his black Converse, arms swinging. His casual body language lets me know that this is a good day for Andrew, and nothing makes me happier.

THE MOVIES

Andrew and I watch a lot of movies together in our family room, him on one side of the couch, me on the other. I try to ignore the strong smell of his feet because I am simply happy that he is upstairs with me, enjoying time together. One night, I show him, "The Slums of Beverly Hills," a movie I have seen multiple times and love for its hilarious ensemble acting. It is the story of a family on the outs, raised by a father, played by Alan Arkin, who never has enough money. They stay in an apartment for a short time until the money runs out, and then they quickly escape without paying, all to be repeated at the next apartment. Because the script and the acting are so good, I laugh out loud, not considering the serious implications of this dark comedy. Andrew does not laugh at all.

At the end of the movie, they once again run out of their apartment when the Alan Arkin character offends his older brother, who has been giving him money to get by. Now they truly have no place to live, and no prospects. The kids try to cheer their father up by saying, "Let's go to Sizzler!" where they will presumably get pancakes and steak, as they always do. When the movie is over, I ask Andrew how he liked it, and he says, "What is going to happen to them now?" Andrew sees this comedy through a lens of compassion, and he worries about them, knowing life will only get harder for them as time goes on, which sadly is the case for him, too. I am stunned. I admire his wisdom in the moment, but as I relive this conversation now, I see in a painful way that he understands that when things get tough for people, they don't always survive.

I often worry that I fail Andrew for my own lack of wisdom, but I know he does not want me to think that way. He wants me to hold my head up, to not look down, and to know that even the toughest times will subside. We will get through the scary rides, and somewhere out there, we will find a quiet place to eat and be nourished without anything frightening us.

I'M SORRY I LEFT YOU

The dream opens with Jim, Andrew, and me standing in a nondescript white ranch home that is situated on a very busy four-lane road, two lanes going each way. Andrew is twenty-four. He screams at us that his life is over, and he runs out of the house, jumps into a large white sedan, and takes off at a high speed, purposefully going the wrong way. I watch the car turn the corner and out of sight as Jim and I jump into our own car and follow him. As we come around the corner, we see the car on the side of the road, its entire roof blasted and peeled open as if a rocket exploded from inside, smashing its way through the top of the car and flying straight up into the heavens. My first thought is, Where's Andrew? *as I look around and see only the car itself. With no signs of his having died at this spot, my second thought is confusion*: There is no way he survived this. *Then my phone rings. I put it to my ear, and I hear Andrew's voice speak to me clearly:*

I'm sorry, Mom.

I'm sorry I left you.

I'm sorry I did this to you.

Then I wake up.

There is a lot here to unpack.

A yoga teacher once tells me that our car is a symbol of our body, our self, our life.

When Andrew drives the car the "wrong way," it is because he can't continue the "same way" as everyone else on the highway of life, and he has no choice but to go the other way, the fatal way. There is no hesitation in his journey. When the car smashes out of sight, I don't see the collision, just as I don't observe *him* zooming straight up to the cosmos, to God, to the Source, blasting through his earthly "container" or shell of a car.

Although the image of the blasted-out car reveals his swift and tragic departure, the dream ends on a sweet note because I *hear* his actual voice, one that feels empathy for me, on a son-to-mother level. This is incredibly healing: my wise, spiritual son is aware of what his actions cost me, his grief-stricken mother.

FIND THE MUSTARD SEED

The police look for a letter that morning, but they can't find it, so we don't look for it either. We assume he didn't write one, which leaves us with mixed feelings. A year and a half later, we are sorting through some boxes in his room when I find a blue, flimsy backpack on the ground from the small college that he didn't attend for very long. For some reason, I pick it up and start patting it down; if it is empty, I will probably throw it out.

I feel what must be a small packet of papers inside. I unzip the front pouch of the backpack and carefully take out a folded letter with Andrew's handwriting on the outside. I read the first line out loud, and Jim stops me, warning me that this is THE letter. We jump in the car to read it by the lake, rather than in our home, but this makes no difference. It is devastatingly sad, and I won't share the contents because the words are meant for our eyes and broken hearts only. But I will share the words that he wrote on the outside of the folded letter: "Mom, go find the mustard seed."

I know what the reference is, but I am awestruck that he knows this specific Buddhist parable and is addressing it to me, specifically. The story refers to a grieving mother who brings the body of her young son from house to house, begging her neighbors for medicine to bring him back to life. A neighbor tells her to bring her son to the Buddha to ask if he has a way. When she brings him to Buddha, he tells her to go back to the village and gather a mustard seed from each neighbor who has not been touched by death. She is eager to do so, but every one of her neighbors cannot give her a mustard seed, because they, too, have been touched by the death of a loved one. She realizes the universality of death and the nature of impermanence. She reports back to the Buddha, and she becomes enlightened; a bodhisattva.

Andrew sometimes makes fun of my fascination with Buddhism, seeing it as an appropriation of culture. But he must have been reading Buddhist texts on his own as he received short books as gifts, and his knowing this parable means that he knew more about Buddhism than I thought. What do I make of his sharing these words via this story in what was among his final moments?

I think he is saying, "Mom, don't be overly distraught. Everyone dies, and everyone experiences loss, and there is not a person to be found anywhere who has not been touched by grief." In this letter, he takes the role of the Buddha by telling me to "find the mustard seed" and ultimately accept the impermanence of life.

Yes, that is very wise, dear boy. I won't go looking for the mustard seed to bring you back, but I will look for you elsewhere—in a deer, dragonfly, and cardinal. It is also still too early in my grieving process, so I won't be enlightened any time soon if and when I ever accept this lesson as the grieving mother does in the parable.

I acknowledge my son's wisdom in his last note of moral support to his sad, tired old mom who is mad about the impermanence of life. I may not be able to access this level of perspective, but I remain open to my spiritual growth, however slowly it comes.

BODHISATTVA

I am standing in front of a large town green, reminiscent of the center of Concord, Massachusetts, dressed in yoga clothes, holding my cat Joey on my right hip, who is wiggling in my arms. He is a large, orange-and-white tabby, one that Andrew is not fond of, a fact that I find ironic later in the dream. I explain to a large group of people that I will be teaching a yoga class as I point to the right corner of the park at the far end of the square. A handful follow me as I walk over the town green to get set up for my class.

I take my usual seated, cross-legged position, place Joey next to me where I can feel his furry body against my right knee, and I begin the warmup with arms reaching out to my sides on an inhale. On the exhale, I feel that a human knee has replaced the furry body of Joey, and I turn my head to see that my cat is gone and is now Andrew, sitting cross-legged and looking right at me, relaxed. In this visitation, he is dressed like a Buddha; in fact, he wears the exact draping of clothes that my twelve-inch Buddha statue wears at home. Andrew's beatific face and exposed chest and heart are turned toward me. I am so delighted to see him, and he looks at me with direct eye contact and a handsome, peaceful face as he communicates telepathically, "Do you want to keep seeing Andrew?" I am stunned by this question and answer emphatically, "Yes, I want to keep seeing you! I see you now, and I see you all the time, so yes, yes, yes!" He responds, enigmatically, "Andrew died this morning." He smiles at me as I slowly wake up.

In reliving the details of this visitation, I recall how Andrew's knee physically touches mine; he makes direct eye contact with me; he is dressed like a Buddha; he acts as my bodhisattva; and he confirms what I want to know—that I will keep seeing him.

And when he says to me, "Andrew died this morning," I interpret this to mean that his Spirit in the afterlife does not identify so closely with the earthly soul he once was. The shamanic healer tells us that Andrew thinks of himself as the "Soul formerly known as Andrew," words that make me smile—I had taken Andrew to a Prince exhibit at the Museum of Pop Culture in Seattle a year before his death.

Andrew is a universal soul, and he can now take many forms. Because we have a strong love and bond for each other, he continues to show up for me, reaching out on many levels, including his newest spiritual self on the Other Side, always knowing when I need to see *him.* It is beautiful and healing for me to experience. I am so touched that he asked me if want to keep seeing him.

Of course, I do.

Always.

PART IV

GRIEF

BACK TO EDEN

We assume Andrew's junior year of college will start out well. During his freshman and sophomore years, he plays volleyball outside his dorm and pickup basketball at the gym, and he is a member of the juggling club. He heads to Vermont with the ski club and enjoys the après ski parties, recanting fun college stories such as how a girl grinds against him in the bar ("Awesome!" is my reaction), how a kid pours beer off the balcony into his mouth, and how one night while he is in a shared bedroom, his bunkmates start telling jokes and they can't stop laughing.

This is going to work, we believe, and we hope. He is a regular college kid, engaging in regular college activities!

He wants a job on campus and finds one easily washing dishes in the dining hall. He makes friends with his work buddies. He earns mostly As and Bs in his demanding coursework.

In his third year, however, he becomes distraught about not passing organic chemistry, a weed out course for pre-med students. After he earns a D- the first time, he convinces himself that he is ready to take it again, the very next semester. This is when I recognize his grit may not serve him well, and I beg him to take more time before jumping in again. He refuses. Although he gets closer to passing with a D+, he unfortunately does not pass the class with the necessary C-. This is a serious blow to his self-esteem, and in addition to living in the biggest party dorm on campus (against our wishes), he is starting to withdraw and become isolated from others. He quits his dining hall job, stating that it bothers his hands, and now he no longer has any kids to interact with. After his junior year, he lets us know he is ready to leave the pressure cooker environment of the big university. We see he is struggling not only with tougher academic expectations of the pre-med program but also with an increasing depression and anxiety due to social isolation.

We arrange a transfer to a smaller university, one that is much closer to home and with supports that seem much easier to access, but he shows no joy in the change. He develops procrastination about his work, which he never had before. As he struggles finding his footing in his new college, his dog Alison is diagnosed a third time with cancer, and I will always question that dreadful decision to put her down.

Shortly after losing his beloved dog, Andrew leaves the second college and lets us know he is ready to enter the work world. We are thrilled about his decision. He interviews at three locations before a kind manager at a Home Depot hires him on the spot. For the next five months, Andrew drives himself back and forth to work with no complaints, no matter the hours, with some shifts starting at 5:00 a.m. and others ending at midnight. He does well. He is a hard worker, conscientious and responsible, and he earns more money than he ever has. He also earns an award for being a great employee, and when I stop by to see him at work, I think to myself, *Who is this handsome, confident young man with a short waist apron, jeans, collared blue golf shirt, and walkie talkie?* I ask him to help me find a certain kind of plant, and he brings me right to it, and then he hustles away—one of his job duties is loading merchandise into cars, and he is called to action. I am so happy and proud of him: a man who hits the road early in the morn and drives himself home late at night, all to do what needs to be done. He tells me he chose Home Depot because he finds it "nostalgic"—they donated the wood he used for his Eagle Project, and he is proud of working for the same company that helped him at one point.

One morning I hear him taking a shower moments before his morning shift, and when I yell that he is going to be late for work, he answers through the bathroom door that he is not going back—that he quit. I protest, I argue, I plead: "You can't just 'quit'! You can't just not show up! That's not how it's done!" But that is that. Jim drives to the store to explain that Andrew is grieving the loss of his thirteen-year-old dog, and his manager states they will hold his job open for one year. Andrew never returns.

We learn later that he was spooked by a helicopter watching him jaywalk while getting the carts. His anxiety about helicopters hovering above him never leaves him from that point on.

We watch as his dreams start floating away out to sea, cruelly, one by one. The dream of being a medical student;

the dream of being an EMT, for which he earns his certification yet has a hard time passing the interview process; the dream of finishing his BS in chemistry with one year left; the dream of working a full-time job, and the disillusionment of the *entire* American dream Andrew constructed as his reward for becoming a doctor—a beautiful wife, a mansion, and a fancy car. He stops driving his blue Honda CRV, which sits in the garage, untouched. He stays at home and remains mostly downstairs pacing the halls or reading long novels in his comfortable brown suede chair. I start driving him to all of his appointments—therapy, psychiatry, ABA (Applied Behavior Analysis), and neurofeedback (mindfulness training using moving images on a screen).

Sadly, none of it is enough to turn back the clock.

I was trying to do all I could, but it still wasn't enough. I don't entirely blame myself. There *isn't enough skilled help readily available to us on this planet* to save this young, handsome man who suffers from the challenge of autism, depression, and anxiety.

The shamanic healer tells us that Andrew came to the earth with a mission: To hold up a harsh mirror to all the systems that don't work—the mental health system, the medical system, and the educational system. Although I make a change when a mental health professional is not working out for him, I can never find the right therapist nor psychiatrist to make the difference in helping Andrew turn the corner. They just aren't in the area where we live for an illness as serious as Andrew's. Or, maybe there is someone who could have helped him, but for whatever reason, I do not know how to find them.

At the same time, Andrew is not an ideal therapy patient. He doesn't share having a plan for self-harm, nor does he share the darkest of his thoughts with anyone, except perhaps in code. One therapist puts together reams of paperwork for him to enter a therapeutic day program well-known for treating depression, but unbeknownst to us, Andrew calls the center and takes himself off the waiting list. When I press him *why* he would do this, when we worked so hard to get him into the program, he is cagey, dodgy, and uncommunicative.

Did he have us fooled that he would soldier on? Or were we fooling ourselves? I notice that none of his therapists want to open that Pandora's box, even when I bring it up directly. I try to pry more out of him when he says something even remotely worrisome, but he clams up and walks away. After Andrew's death, Jim makes the horrifying discovery that he was interacting with others on the dark web, which gives my grief an even-beyond place to go.

The night before he leaves us, Andrew and I are watching a show on Netflix—a flippant comedy that takes place in the afterlife, saddest of ironies—and I note he is more relaxed than usual. His six-foot-one body is sprawled long out across the couch, and his bare feet are close to me, but they are not as smelly as usual as he scrolls through his phone while I watch the show. The moment feels calm in our quiet companionship. When the show concludes and I get up from the couch to head to bed, he stands up and presses his back against the wall near the exit of the family room, which is not usual for him. I make eye contact with him and say casually but warmly, "Good night, Andrew." He looks right into my eyes, and quietly says, "Good night." I believe at that moment he knows it will be our last, and that is why he makes sustained eye contact with me, not something he ordinarily does.

Later that week, I find his phone plugged in and resting on the arm of the couch. Like most of us, his phone is always by his side. I find it perplexing that he makes the decision to leave his phone behind when he goes downstairs for the last time. We are never able to access it; we do not have his password.

I sense that *for him,* leaving us is something he follows through to escape a constant, endless cycle of deep pain, relentless depression, and the loss of his dreams. I visualize angels immediately arriving on each side of him, tall, statuesque, God-like males with benevolent, neutral faces, holding him up and zooming him out of his body and back to Source, back to Eden. I see him being welcomed by his beloved dog Alison, and by Grandpa Donald, Poppy, Uncle Quin, and all the cool rock stars that he adores who went before him: David Bowie, Prince, and Ric Ocasek of The Cars. I think of him wide-eyed and in a state of wonder when he sees, hears, and experiences what the afterlife has in store for him. He is happy, he is free, he is exploring, and he is not in pain. He is no longer ill.

My therapist says that Andrew had cancer of the soul, and yet most people don't think of it that way. They don't know how to acknowledge the deep, unrelenting pain of the depressed, nor do they even see it. I saw it every day. I didn't know how to make it go away.

My own depression often crushes my heart and soul into tiny fragments and pieces. Even three years later, I am often hit by a tsunami of sadness. I hope one day I may learn how to accept his decision. He returns to the place where the sun, the moon, the stars, and the galaxies shine for him every day, and for that much I can be glad.

GRIEF, BLAME, GUILT, ACCEPTANCE

Grief complicated by blame. My therapist, husband, family members, friends, and shamanic healer have all told me, sternly: This is *not* your fault. On an analytical level, I agree. I nod my head silently. *It's not my fault.* And I have worked very hard to get to a place where I can see all the pieces of *his* own life that brought Andrew to the place he arrived to. The shamanic healer says that everyone is responsible for their own journey and thus their own choices. It's still damn hard not to blame myself when I lose my son in my own house.

I have always been a truth teller—and that is a lonely place to be. And the hard truth is, I am not a perfect mother. I am a jerk. I lose my temper. I am often enraged and hurt and humiliated and angry and frightened and overwhelmed and nasty and mean. I say things that I wish were never said. So has Andrew. But I also know that he forgives me just as I forgive him. The shamanic healer tells us there is "nothing to forgive," and that Andrew is grateful for all we did for him—and a little embarrassed about how he often treated us. For some reason, any time that he did not treat me well is completely forgotten on my end. His forgiveness of me feels true; it's just hard for me to let it stick, and to let it absolve me.

When the detective who is with us for two hours or so says she has never seen parents who did more than we did for their son, I still can't 100 percent believe it. It's true I am *always* looking for answers, and then moving on when *that* didn't work out to find *new* answers from the next round of therapists, psychiatrists, life coaches, rehab counselors for employment, and social workers. We fight hard with a lawyer and mediator on our side to make sure Andrew spends his last two years of high school at a small, private, expensive, "therapeutic" school where we hope he will make real friends, which we finance through a 401(k) loan to subsidize what the public school offers on their end. It also takes us years to pay off our portion of the psychiatric stay at Boston's Children's Hospital. We pay out of pocket for his neurofeedback appointments and light treatments for his vitiligo, a loss of skin pigment, just another thing that he must deal with. I never regret spending a penny on him for anything. We are just eternally sad because we are left with the nagging feeling that there was something we missed—that if *only* we had found the right school, psychiatrist, therapist, and medication combination, we could stop the elusive foe of advancing mental illness in its tracks.

But forgiveness must enter our hearts. I am not perfect, neither is Jim. We are not perfect parents, and yet we must forgive ourselves, if for no other reason than we are only human, and humans make mistakes. What we lack in perfect parenting we make up for with fierce love, a love that won't quit, a protective love that means we will fight for him, a love that wakes me up every morning ready to try something new, a love that is on the lips of my every birthday wish before blowing out the candles, and a love that is sent to the first person I think of when I practice *Metta,* the Buddhist practice of loving kindness, knowing that he needs it the most. *May Andrew be happy. May Andrew be healthy. May Andrew be free from suffering. May he be at peace.* Always wishing, hoping, praying, striving, and believing that Andrew will get better, that Andrew will get well, that Andrew will be able to live alongside this foe and ultimately be its warrior.

Grief complicated by guilt. There is the sense that maybe there *is* one thing that tips the scales in the wrong direction at this or that moment in time, like employers not getting back to him on his latest requests for an interview. Or maybe it is me, because I get lazy and don't fight hard enough to change up his most recent therapist and psychiatrist – I know they are not fighting for *him* hard enough, but we had just switched, and I do not have the energy to switch *again* in lieu of finding the *next* therapist and psychiatrist to try *their* "magic." Maybe we should have moved to somewhere else in the US where Andrew would have been even more comfortable, as we did when we left an urban environment to one that was more rural. Should we have kept trying, again, and then again? We did. And we would have *kept on* trying. But we didn't know. We are just sad.

Even as I write about my intertwined grief, pain, and blame, there are two things that need some light to be shed upon—how Andrew, in his spirit form, feels about my self-recrimination and our ultimate acceptance of what has come to pass. Can *I* just allow myself to move toward self-forgiveness? Stop the blaming? Why *do* I continue to beat myself up when that is not what *Andrew* wants?

I have many visitations, dreams, and signs that indicate a playfulness, sweetness, closeness, gratitude, and willingness to be my spiritual guide. I am brought to my knees in awe, to tears and smiles of joy, to a paradise in the clouds from an abyss of complex depression. I regularly see and hear from him as the bright, brassy swish of a cardinal with its piercing *pyu, pyu;* through the deeply soulful eyes of a young deer; by the stubborn, perky dragonfly that parks himself on a thin branch and sits with me or alights on my thumb; and a hawk watching me from a tree, followed by circling overhead. Andrew reveals the heavens themselves as I look up to see them rolled back for me to get a glimpse. And yet, despite all these gifts, I still fall, flail, and fight off the blues with sticks—and cling to the cruel notion that I failed him.

It is wonderful beyond words to see Andrew in spiritual forms, AND it is heartbreaking to be faced with the no-holds-barred, bare-boned fact that the young man I loved here on this planet is farther away from me than I ever would have thought. I have to hold both of these things as true—and that is a tricky juggling act.

My therapist reminds me, and I remind Jim, in turn, that we need to move toward acceptance, because it is what Andrew wants—as well as honoring the choice he made, as a warrior in his own right. He was in a pain so deep, far deeper than any bouts I have had. A loneliness that boils up to a scream and a howl, so lonely is he for someone other than his parents to *get* him, to love him, to be with him, just as he is. I can bounce back from a hard day, or days, or a week, to where I can find some comfort in eating a home-cooked meal, snuggling with my cat Shelby, or checking out from life for a while, watching something mindless on Netflix. After ups and downs and merry-go-rounds of thirty-five years of marriage, I can relax in sharing my life with Jim—in fact, it is the simpler things that now give me the greatest joy and ease in my life. Walking in nature or sitting on my deck to listen to birds and the high-pitched twinkle of my dragonfly chimes with the sun on my face and a drink nearby is my idea of bliss.

But if you ask me right now, even in my most relaxed moments, if I accept what happened, my chest tightens up—which means I am not ready for acceptance. And of course not. Right now, it has been ten months, and his room still looks pretty close to what it did after our first attempt to organize, with his much-used backpack slouched and abandoned on the floor, his bureau filled to the brim with underwear, socks, band T-shirts, many pairs of jeans from Old Navy, long basketball-style running shorts, track pants, and Lego sets put together one last time—only partially still together, having been knocked around by the cats—a fact that doesn't bother him one bit anymore. I am not even close to being ready to deal with sorting and making decisions about all the things that were part of who he was while he was with us on this earth. And almost three years later, not much has changed. The room still looks like someone left in a hurry, and nobody else is able to deal with it.

Not long after his funeral, I come up with a grand idea: a road trip in an RV with the urn. All over the US, California, and Hawaii. Then Sedona. Or just California. Then all of it, canceled. For now. Just not ready. I can't accept he is gone, and making a decision with his ashes is not something I can do.

But when I am ready, I will accept what happened. But until then, maybe I can move on to self-forgiveness. Or at least really work on it.

Andrew would like that.

TO TELL OR NOT

As we finish the reception luncheon of sandwiches, chips, and natural sodas after the funeral, separated by six feet in my backyard on separate chairs, Jim and I wave goodbye to immediate family members as they drive away. My neighbor, who is walking his tiny dog down the street, sees us and asks congenially, "Have a good party?" We tell him we just had a gathering—and this is why. He tears up, looks visibly upset, apologizes profusely, turns around with his dog, and goes home. He is a good support to us, and a few days later, his wife brings over a blueberry crumble that brings me tears of joy because it tastes so good and we are both in need of something good. Our neighbors support us with treats, flowers, and plants. I am glad they all know. We live in a small neighborhood, and I prefer everyone knows upfront without my having to pretend nothing happened.

Outside of the neighborhood, I sometimes just blurt it out. The world better hear this, goddamn it! The day before Andrew's funeral, a florist is bitchy to me about how the flowers I SAID I wanted were different from what I am saying

NOW. She says in a nasty voice as she replaces the flowers, "You should have told me."

"These are for my son's funeral. He died two days ago. He took his life." So yeah, I told her.

On a dreary fall day during COVID times, Jim and I walk quietly through an unfamiliar neighborhood for a change of scenery. A raspy, disembodied female voice speaks from inside the house we are passing, hissing to us that we are "Losers!" for not wearing masks. Lady, we are outside, walking in a public neighborhood where there is no one around, and if there *was* someone there, we would of course put on our masks. We turn around to leave, clearly feeling unwelcome, and as we walk away, Jim suddenly turns and screams the full news at her. That makes her shut up. Message to earthlings: Don't ever assume the person in front of you is doing OK, by default. I look at myself from others' eyes, and say in my head, *They have no idea*. Or they may have lost someone too, or if they haven't yet, they will lose someone, soon enough. We all have or will lose someone we love. We need to take it easy on our fellow humans because of that.

I think there is no right or wrong about telling or not telling. I give myself a pass if I decide to tell in an abrupt way, or *not* to tell at all. None of it is planned out in advance—it just fits the moment, or the moment passes. And more than once, if someone gives me shit that I can't handle, I will tell them what happened to me to remind them to back off and be nice to me. I think that's fair.

I start to tell certain friends by sending a card first with the sad news, and then waiting to get a phone call. Then I just stop. It seems like telling too many people, or telling people that I haven't seen for a long time, is just too much for me, as if my heart can only open *this much* before it must shut its door for a while and exist on standby mode.

And I think that's OK.

THE FIRST BIRTH DAY

Andrew has been gone eight and a half months; March 8, 2021, would have been his twenty-fifth birthday. Jim and I make a carefully structured plan to take the day off work and go to the Cape.

In my mind, I am calling it his "*birth* day," rather than "birthday" to take out any expectation of celebrating. The plan is a good one on paper: walking the Sandwich Beach during the day, listening to Andrew's favorite music in the car (The Cars, Huey Lewis) as we drive, and ending with a home-cooked grilled salmon dinner followed by a small ice cream cake. We will Zoom call with our daughter Michaela, who lives in DC. Grieving during COVID.

We are bundled up in layers. I am under my puffy blue North Face coat while Jim is wearing Andrew's black North Face coat that his son wore a year ago. There is a steady cold wind as we stagger across a very rocky beach, eyes squinting into the white-tip, whipped waves and weak sunshine. The mood on the beach is a bit uplifting because it is bracing, but Jim is struggling, and it suddenly feels biting, sad, and confusing. How are we supposed to feel here, a place we often visited as a family of four? At one point, Jim says, "This is not working for me," so we leave the cold oceanfront to head back to the car. We walk alongside a briskly moving saltwater river that leads through a marsh to a bridge, where once upon a time, the four of us got brave for a single moment and jumped off the banister, inspired by locals, into the icy cold depths below. Now, it's just Jim and I walking quietly on the long, familiar, narrow boardwalk over the marshes, reading the planks as we step, carved with names and hearts in memory of loved ones.

We eat our sandwiches in the car and then head to Hyannis, listening to The Cars—the first time since Andrew left us that I allow myself to play his favorite rock band. I totally understand why he loves them so much, with their coolness, ability to fit the moment, bold, in-your-face-but-in-a-good-way refrains, and cut-to-the-chase lyrics.

At the same time, music is easily triggering. I often come home from the gym gasping and crying as I burst through the garage door to collapse on the kitchen floor, all because I was playing too many songs that remind me of Andrew in a place where I see him working out on weights and the rowing machine. The lyrics, oh god, the lyrics, how they oddly refer so often to the singer's need to leave it all behind, because they *need* to leave.

We arrive at a small, nearly empty beach in Hyannis with the memory of bringing our lithe, blond, fun kids there on a summer's day. They played in the shallow, child-friendly stream that empties its waters into welcoming waves that lap lightly onto soft sand. The sun comes out in fuller force, and we don't need bulky coats anymore as we take a slow walk next to the water, eventually sitting on the sand to watch boxy buffleheads and sleek cormorants gliding on top of the water. *Sloop!* Suddenly the cormorants are nowhere to be seen, although we know they are under the surface. Like Andrew. This beach is kinder to our raw emotions as we talk about light things and allow the sun to do its magic on our vulnerable faces and bruised hearts. Shorebirds fly overhead, swim, and dive underwater without a sound, only to pop up again. Forever buoyant.

Driving home at the end of day, we listen to Huey Lewis and the News with the front man's exuberant man-boy voice, the sax solos, and the bright harmonies and melodies of his band members. It works to cheer me up as I remember Andrew's request only last year that we listen to "Do you Believe in Love?" when visiting my friend Susie at her home on Camano Island in Washington State. She says, "Great choice, Andrew," and she blasts it: Sunroof open, windows down, car zooming across the rural, farm-like, island countryside, the two of us singing loudly and joyfully in the front while Andrew sits in the backseat, quiet but taking it all in.

But then all the joy in our own car ceases to be, and the singing and clapping eight months after his death feels forced. I am tired and want to be home and see our kitties, who have become our children. The grieving process feels like a ping-pong ball: I am whacked around, seemingly having fun, flying lightly through the air, until someone or something hits me hard with a paddle and I go down. Hard. *Ouch.*

The salmon dinner we prepare is delicious—but of course, it doesn't feel the same. Why would it? I miss Andrew eating his salmon by bringing his face close to the plate, shoveling it into his mouth, and slurping down the juices. We position ourselves on the couch to look at our daughter's face projected on the flat TV, and we each have our ice-cream cake desserts on both sides of the screen. I suggest we *not* sing "Happy Birthday"; instead, I light a single candle, and we say, one at a time, "I love you, Andrew." I am nervous about being triggered—the sudden onset of intense chest pain—but I surprise myself by making it through the birthday cake ritual in one piece. You never know when the brain will decide to send pain to the heart.

Jim, however, is just barely holding back a flood of tears. This is a good thing. He doesn't cry as much or as often as me, but he *needs* to, grieving father, and if he cries on Andrew's birthday, well, of course. In this very moment, I feel oddly buoyed by the day. Being by the ocean tends to be healing for me.

It is the *next* twenty-three days of March that have me in tears, in chest pain, slapped around, exhausted emotionally, and wondering what the hell happened to him, to me, to us, to all of us. I am never so happy to see April 1 arrive, and for Easter, I buy Andrew a chocolate Reese's bunny, propping it up in his cabinet, not too far away from his Reese's Valentine heart.

FRIDAY NIGHT PIZZA

Friday night pizza with olives and feta cheese, side of root beer. Grilled salmon dinners with baked potato and sour cream. Falafel sandwich wrap. Angel hair pasta and marinara sauce. Linguini with tomatoes and basil. Clam chowder with oyster crackers. Guacamole and chips. Parmesan Goldfish. Egg and sausage breakfast sandwiches. Homemade waffles on Sunday mornings.

Our tall, skinny Andrew loves to eat. And drink. Milk by tall glassfuls, one after the other; we can barely keep the fridge stocked with six half-gallons. Later on, grape soda. Orange mango pineapple juice. Raspberry lime rickey.

Which leads me to his favorite desserts, starting with crème brûlée. Soft-serve vanilla with rainbow sprinkles. Caramel Frappuccino from Starbucks. Friendly's ice cream cake, but only on his birthday. Ben and Jerry's chocolate chip cookie dough. Oreos. Boston cream donuts from Dunkin.'

Making sure he has his favorite foods is the one thing I can do *really well* as Andrew's mother. No matter how late it is, tired I am from work, or inconvenient the ride, walking into the house with a hot pizza from the car is well worth the investment . . . because he *wants* it. Seeing him dice garlic and smash the avocadoes in a small bowl in the kitchen—then stepping aside to allow me to dip my tortilla chip in his guacamole—is a promise for his future, and in that moment, all is right with the world.

Grocery shopping afterward is horrible. It gets better as I numb out, but in the early days and weeks of grieving, I lose it in the pasta aisle: stuck, standing in place, vision blurring as I stare unsteadily at the horizontally stacked pasta boxes, not making sense of what is in front of me. If not in front of the pasta, then the frozen aisle, where his favorite Amy's cheese enchiladas are found, or the dairy case, with its cheeses and yogurts that ultimately send me running to the car, crying, getting smacked in the face with the hard reality that wherever you are in the universe, Andrew, you don't need me to get food for you anymore.

I used to text him, "Hi Andrew, I'm at Whole Foods. Is there anything you want?"

Waiting for the dot, dot, dot, followed by a lengthy list—Andrew & Everett Swiss cheese, Mary's Gone Crackers, Aussie Greek vanilla yogurt—and I make sure I get *everything*, even if it means running all over the store. Once I can't find the right hot chocolate brand, so I improvise and find a different one and a bag of marshmallows on the side, and when I get home, I explain the reason for the alternative. He looks me in the face and says, "Well done." I feel as if I have won a gold medal.

Praise is hard to come by, and Andrew is a man of few words. Store-bought birthday cards are simply signed, "Love,

Andrew," but sometimes accompanied by a small, hand-drawn heart. Any loving words from him are treasured. I don't expect him to emote with gratitude when I shop for him—his eating the food *is* the thank you—but the occasional positive comment makes my entire day. When he is angry, upset, disappointed—with me, his dad, the world—I painfully realize how much this planet has let him down in so many ways. I cry, outwardly and inwardly, with rage in my heart, knowing that in those moments, there is nothing else I can do to make him happy, or make his world better.

The weeks leading up to the night that he leaves us, he stops asking for specific things from the store. When I text him to ask if he needs anything, he texts back a hard, simple, "NO." There used to be a time when he shops with me, dropping multiple items in the cart, his favorites piling up, and I do not care one iota about the price or if it is a healthy choice. Big thick ice cream sandwiches, even though we already have sandwich crème cookies, a four pack of gourmet root beer, and a pint of Ben and Jerry's—Sure! Throw it in! What matters to me is that these food favorites *matter* to him. I am crushed when he doesn't care about any of his favorites anymore.

In the Pixar movie "Soul," the reluctant Soul 22 played by Tina Fey has not incarnated and has no interest in Earth, until she does so and tries pizza for the first time and realizes how amazingly rich and good it is as a sensory experience. As I reflect on all the pizzas my boy ate while he was with us, I face the reality that even his favorite Friday night pizza with olives and feta, swished down with a hearty swallow of cold root beer, is not enough to keep him here with us.

YEAR TWO: GRIEF AND GRACE

No one tells me that Year Two of grieving will be worse than Year One. I find this out for myself pretty quickly.

Year One for us is about following a belief system that the best way to approach grieving is to go to work, stay busy, dedicate oneself to a purpose, get out of the house, and when home, distract yourself. We are in the middle of a pandemic and hunkered down in the evenings after work as the days grows shorter. Jim wipes the groceries down and we cook, rather than talk about Andrew too much. We sit close together on the couch to watch entertaining shows that are not triggering, serious, nor sad. We watch the daily news about COVID, and I create lesson plans for 100-percent remote teaching at first, followed by hybrid, and then in-person while wearing a mask the whole time, which feels like a metaphor. Yes, I am grieving, but also "remotely" until a visceral trigger crosses my consciousness, and then I melt down: racing out of stores, curling up in the car, stumbling into the house after listening to a song that hit too close to home, burying my face in a flannel pillow for screams to be roared into. Year One meltdowns.

Year Two involves my questioning Year One's coping systems. Year Two includes the grocery store and song triggers, but what is added is a numbing depression and feeling physically as if new heart crevices are being carved. There is a slowly clenching fist in my chest that doesn't let go of my already beaten-up heart—and panic attacks still make an appearance. I go through the motions by working out, going outside in nature, taking short walks in the neighborhood, ten-minute morning meditations, and taking yoga classes online, but I also retreat to my messy, never-made bed to hide under multiple fleece blankets, seeking softness to take the edge off the world. Getting up out of bed in the mornings is nearly impossible—it is a *Force yourself!* command on my part to do it.

In Year One, I don't know it, but I am in shock. I live and breathe inside a protective bubble of denial that allows me to cry when I need to cry and fall apart when I need to fall apart, but these incidents are sharp and short-lived. I never cry at work, but I take naps on my yoga mat, even falling completely asleep during a prep period with a timer on my phone to wake me up—the exhaustion of trying to look and be normal. The unimaginable has happened, but I am somehow able to stop up my grief to wait for afterwork hours.

The English teacher in me has the blessing and the curse of teaching about characters in literary works who experience loss, death, violence, and grief. This is all while thousands upon thousands are losing their lives from COVID as I am processing my own grief. And I see it, and I acknowledge it, and I know objectively that I will come home every day to a much quieter house, but I keep these facts on separate shelves.

With the anniversary of Andrew's death looming ahead, we book a long weekend in a nice hotel near the southwestern Rhode Island beaches. Rhode Island beaches have no memories for us; we have never taken our kids there, so there are no triggers. But along with a few creeping, dark clouds here and there, the dearth of grief moves into my heart as we drive from the hotel to a beach.

It is a cloudy afternoon in Narragansett, and I am angry and sad for no reason and for all the reasons. I tell Jim to pull over, I get out of the car, and I start walking up the highway to I don't know where. It is lightly but alarmingly raining on my face, the sky is dark, and because I hopped out of the car quickly, I have no cell phone. I just want to cry and walk, with no plan. After fifteen minutes, Jim finds me and pulls over. We head back to the semi-high-rise hotel, and we sit in our room with its cathedral ceilings and territorial view, looking out on the clouds and the sun setting. We just feel very, very sad. Thus begins Year Two.

And yet, on our last day in Rhode Island, we receive a gift of love and unexpected grace. We go to a takeout seafood place at Port Judith, and the line is excruciatingly long. This is during a brief time that summer when masks are off, but we are still socially distancing by standing on marks on the ground when waiting in lines. There comes a point when we don't know whether to bail or just stay put in line when a very nice young man in front of us, a native Rhode Islander, starts chatting in that very friendly way some twenty-year-olds have who are more mature than most. He assures us that the food is so good that it is worth the wait. He is a contractor who has just started his own business, and he is proud that he recently completed the siding of this very restaurant whose takeout window we are slowly inching toward. He shares with us that he had a mentor in his fifties who taught him everything that he knew, and that this man recently died by suicide, and he can't understand why. We are silent. Then I ask the young man his name, and he says, "Ryan." He is twenty-three, and his birthday is March 9.

Andrew's middle name is *Ryan,* he was *twenty-four* when he died on July *23*, and his birthday is March *8*.

As I am processing this, Ryan gets to the window and puts in his order. He then says goodbye to us, gives me his business card, waves, and walks away. When it is our turn to order, the waitress says, "That kid just gave me twenty dollars to go toward your meal."

I start crying and can't stop. I cry while waiting for our order to come out. I cry while eating my clam chowder on a bench under a tent. For a twenty-something to treat a sad, middle-aged couple, who surely make more income than he does; it just feels like the kindest thing anyone can do for us in this moment. I want to thank him, and I look around for him. I suddenly see him jump into his service truck, about to leave the parking lot, so I run up to his window to tell him, "Thank you! Thank you!" And then I fill him in briefly about Andrew. He says, "Oh my god, I didn't know." I say, "Of course, you couldn't have known, but your gesture was just so kind, I will never forget it."

When we lose our Andrew, the flowers, houseplants, phone calls, cards, muffins, and the blueberry crumble warms us up and keeps us going in the moment. When this young man gives twenty dollars of his hard-earned money toward our meal a year later on a day that has no special meaning to him, just to be kind for the sake of being kind, it gives my heart a warm, loving squeeze in a good way, and the tears that fall are happy tears, borne of an unexpected gift.

Year Two in the fall continues to be hard. Working is harder. The grief continues to carve scissures into my poor, sore heart. I can't believe Andrew is gone. "Time heals all wounds" doesn't apply in the case of losing a child. Jim's dad used to say, "Things are never as bad as they seem." We don't believe that line anymore, either; if anything, it seems that things are exactly as bad as they seem. We don't make wishes when we blow the candles on the cake. Why bother wishing? It never worked before.

Now it is April, a week from Easter. Jim used to be the Easter bunny, getting up in the middle of the night to hide the eggs in tricky spots for Michaela and Andrew to find them. The chocolate bunny I bought from CVS is still propped up in Andrew's cabinet above his urn from last year. Oh my god, we are three months away from the second anniversary, which starts Year Three of the grieving process.

How is this possible? All of it is possible. Including Ryan and his twenty-dollar gift of love and compassion to two complete strangers who somehow have a connection with him. The grace of goodness still exists.

PART V

SIGNS AND MIRACLES

THE FIRST DRAGONFLY

The first time I see the dragonfly is the morning of a trip to the Cape. Today is my birthday, six weeks after losing my only son. For an hour as we pack for the beach, a dragonfly solidly perches on the passenger-side car window. He is still and content, just like Andrew was as a baby, watching us as a beloved member of our family. I take a picture and send it out, and my sister Becky texts back to say that she is in a friend's swimming pool, and a dragonfly just landed on her hand. My brother-in-law Dave joins the text chain to say that a dragonfly just hit him in the chest while he was riding his bike. Something is up.

When we turn on the car an hour later, the dragonfly is still there. He only flits away when the car starts to move in reverse down the driveway. We drive toward the Bourne Bridge, stuck in traffic, while a swarm of dragonflies zoom about in the airspace above our car.

This day marks the beginning of our journey with Andrew visiting us in the form of a dragonfly, a spiritual incarnation that he makes easily again and again.

Two months or so later, during a morning commute, Andrew's shy face pops up as a caller on my phone. Such a thing is not possible–his phone is inactive, and we cannot open it. I go to work, teach my classes, and at the end of the day I walk up the set of stairs that lead to an empty parking lot and ask a question to the sky, "Andrew, was that you this morning, on my phone?" The instant I ask, a red dragonfly comes into view on my left, flies right by my face, then far to the right before he circles around. From several feet away, he launches toward me, stops right in front of my face, and does a happy dance two inches away. Then he spirals around one tree, another, the entire roof of the school, then over and out, leaving me breathless and speechless.

I have seen this happy dance before. A few weeks earlier, Jim and I are in the car, getting emotionally ready to pick up Andrew's cremains from the funeral home. Before we leave the house, we sit in the car pensively. I break the silence by saying, "Well, Andrew, are you ready to come home?"

Just like *that,* a dragonfly pops up from the bottom of the car and starts banging itself repeatedly against our windshield, alternating with a crazy, zany, happy dance. We drive to the funeral home with no thoughts or words, other than Jim saying under his breath, "Wow. That was weird."

The dragonfly visits continue. On a fall bike ride by myself, I stop to sit by a stream on a bridge, and right then a small, black-bodied dragonfly sits next to me. We start a two-way conversation. I say, "I love you," and he answers by lifting his little wings in a call and response: "Up down." This goes on for several moments. I am so very happy, sitting next to my son in this little form of nature.

After our very first session with the shamanic healer, Jim and I go on a local Audubon Walk to reflect on a lot of information. We pause on a bridge over a slowly flowing river body with many dragonflies hovering close to the water. One very big, dark-bodied dragonfly flies slowly and methodically right by our faces, twice, so we can really see him, before spiraling up into the trees. Later in the hike, a big, black dragonfly follows us and then suddenly strikes Jim on the cheek. He then perches his giant insect body against a tree, as if saying to us, "Keep looking at me!" Then he flies to my shoulder and rests on the back of my jacket. The rest of the day is filled with dragonflies everywhere we go. It is a very good dragonfly day with Andrew.

But then winter comes. There are no more dragonflies and no signs. Not even cardinals.

We get through by going completely overboard for Christmas with a multitude of lights on the house and around all five of our dogwood trees. We light up and decorate two Christmas trees inside, one for the front window to throw light out into the dark night, and one in the family room across from the cabinet where Andrew's urn sits among mementos. Jim and I take long walks in the winter sun, in the dark, bundled up, looking and searching for answers in the night sky. I'm hoping to dream of him at night. Nothing.

And finally, spring is back. And last weekend we watch our dragonfly-Andrew doing his happy, zany dance once again, coming in close, and then darting away, daring us to follow him, in form and in shadow, only to glide right back into view. We sit on a bank and experience his soul behind my head, above my head, beating his wings away furiously right in front of my face, and buzzing by Jim's ear. He lands on my hand, my shoulder, my back, my thigh, and Jim takes pictures of me sitting in the sun among the warm pine needles.

Welcome back, joyful boy. As joyful as Charlie Bucket singing on stage, but this time, dancing with your transparent, prehistorically engineered, delicate and tough wings that allow you to fly high, fly low, and fly all the way around us. We see you. Fly around your mother and father, who marvel in your spirit, your freedom, and your loving, caring connection to us. Your parents are always searching for you, up in every sky, hidden in every tree, and skating about every lake and pond.

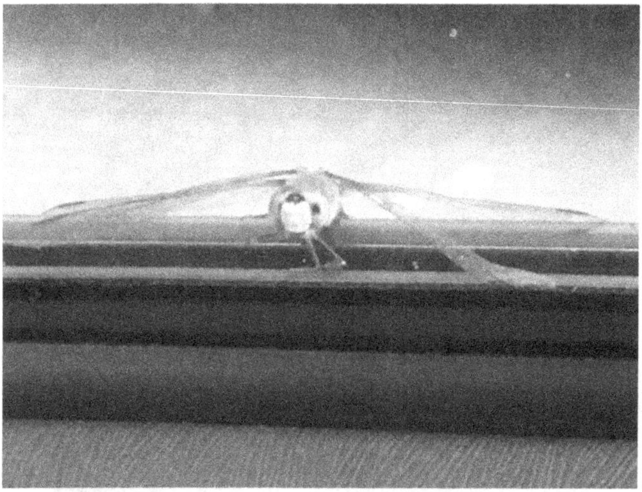

SIGNS

When the chips are down, I reach out to Andrew, and in some form or other, he responds quickly. While driving home from work and feeling very low, I speak out loud to the emptiness in the car, "Andrew, I need a sign." Suddenly, a small square patch of blue bursts through the cloudy gray cover overheard, and by the time I make a right onto my street five minutes later, the patch of sky has transformed into a wondrous, colorful, evolving celestial event. It is a peek into paradise.

I ask for signs a lot the first year while commuting, which is my very focused time of thinking about him. One day, he responds with a piano rendition of the song, "Give Me Your Hand" by George Winston, coming out of the car's speakers, and I cry with surprise and delight. Andrew often resolves mother-son arguments by suddenly offering his hand and uttering one of the last lines from *A Midsummer Night's Dream*: "Give me your hand / and we be friends." The argument would stop as I take his extended hand, feeling the soft, smooth touch of his long fingers in my own.

I ask for a sign from Andrew, my guardian angels, and God. It is a rough morning. Asking for a sign from all these entities couldn't hurt, and I also don't want to overextend Andrew. Less than five minutes later, a *SIGN* literally appears in my vision, off the road on my right, in the form of a billboard I have never seen before. The message is in big, black letters on a white background with a dad holding his blond little son in the air, with the words, "Helping you enjoy the ride. We are with you, by your side." Did I ever need that.

One time I don't ask for a sign, but I receive a rainbow, literally. After a rainy commute home, I walk in the house, glance out the window of my kitchen, and stop in my tracks to behold a fully formed rainbow, end to end, with a sheet of rain in front of it and the woods beyond as the backdrop. Oddly, there is no sun—just the most glittering and sparkling rainbow I've ever seen! I do not move one inch, not even to get my phone, until it gently fades away. This is the best kind of sign, unasked-for, as I live in the moment of the miracle while it shimmers right in front of me.

Andrew seems to know when I am in the darkest of moods with magical signs to keep me believing. I force myself outside for a 5:00 p.m. walk after a bad day, and within seconds, a bright cardinal makes himself known on the highest branch of a tree with the low-lying sun flashing on its red-orange breast, throwing a spotlight for an impromptu concert of birdcalls that echoes through my street for an audience of one. Just today, I come home from the dentist feeling glum, sensing this could be a bad day, and as I walk in the house, the song "It's Magic" by The Cars pops on. I hook up my phone to my Sonos speaker and dance my heart out in the dining room to the bewilderment of my two cats.

I pull up the blinds one morning before work and am startled to see a young deer looking right at me through the window, as if calmly expecting me to look outside at 6:30 a.m. The following summer, early one morning, as I am driving on the roads of New Hampshire on my way to a writer's workshop there is a deer standing in the middle of the road, as if waiting for me to arrive. I slow to a stop, and we just look at each for five minutes before he walks slowly off into the woods.

There are so many signs now—perhaps impossible to document them all. Signs are a daily occurrence in my life, and I hope to share as many as I can while I am still here on this earth to witness, to experience, and to document the magic of Andrew on the Other Side.

THE RED DRAGONFLY

On a sunny Saturday in November, Jim and I take a walk to Pleasure Point, a small, sandy beach by a lake where we go to talk freely about Andrew, when the house feels like too much. There are no cardinals flying around, which makes me sad, because we usually see and hear lots of them. It also seems unlikely we will see many dragonflies today. One magical time, we see a dragonfly and a cardinal both together in the same spot, one that overlooks a water-lily studded marsh, and we are elated. Today, we are mildly hopeful to see a stray dragonfly by the lake this late in the season.

Andrew didn't see much of this town. I hoped he would. When we are in the process of buying the house, I imagine bringing him here to this warm, sunny, pine-carpeted little point of land that includes a small beach facing a clear lake. This never happens, but for some reason, every time we go there, I think of him.

Jim and I sit on a short stone wall when I suddenly see a red dragonfly purposefully land on the beach, sitting stoically while he faces the lake. I point it out to Jim, who has also seen it. I slowly move my body off the wall, walk across the sand, mindful of not blocking the sun as I carefully sit down so we can sit side by side to look at the water and be warm together. Jim says, "Don't scare it off." I won't. I am the dragonfly whisperer. I got this.

After sitting side by side for a few minutes, I reach out to stroke his left wing. The red dragonfly accepts my petting just fine, so I continue, not to overdo, but just gently, gently connecting through touch. I tell Jim to come over, but he's still nervous about scaring it away. He finally comes over, giving the two of us a wide berth. Now we are on two sides of the dragonfly, Jim facing him from the front for a few moments. Suddenly, the red dragonfly lifts himself off the ground, and my first thought is, *Jim's right; we've scared him away*, but this is not the case as he doubles back immediately, heads toward me, and lands on the right thumb of my hand, which is resting in my lap.

"Oh my god," I whisper. This is now the third time a dragonfly has landed on my hand, but this time, it is not because my hand is extended. This is purely his idea.

Jim takes a picture, right away. I look at Jim, and he is smiling.

He is happy. So am I.

The red dragonfly stays for a few more moments. Then gentle as the wind, he leaves my thumb and flies away, to where, I know not.

When I look at the close-up of the dragonfly on my thumb, it looks just like my son. The second photo includes mother with son, with a tender expression and knowingness on my face that it is him.

Andrew asks me in a dream if I want to keep seeing him, and I said, “Yes! And I do see you, all the time!” And here he is. It is true then, what my therapist says: he is always with me.

And on some days, the fact that he visits me as a dragonfly or a cardinal or a deer is enough.

And today, having him land on my thumb with Jim watching is far more than enough.

THE CARDINAL ON CHARLES STREET

"Can you take the car to the shop today for an inspection?"

Jim is referring to Andrew's car—the royal blue 2007 Honda CRV that we bought for Michaela and then passed on to Andrew when she didn't need it anymore as a city girl using public transit in DC. It is a great little car with a five-CD stereo, and I have memories, real and imagined, of Andrew driving himself back and forth across the state to college; in the dark for an early morning shift at Home Depot, and with other college students traveling up north with the ski club, all his favorite CDs loaded up. His sister will re-inherit it when she is ready to leave city life behind, but for now, it stays with us in a cherished place in our two-car garage.

Andrew left us for the Other Side on July 23, 2020. The inspection sticker expired on the last day of August 2020. Today is April 23, 2021. I didn't plan that to be the date when I finally bring it to the shop.

I call before I leave the house, and the guy tells me to make sure I park in the parking lot, *not in front of the bay,* and he will get to my car in *twenty minutes*. I show up, follow his precise directions, and for some compelling reason, I need to tell him why the inspection sticker has been expired for several months. A grizzled, middle-aged, annoyed mechanic sees me from the bay and reluctantly walks into the small reception area to remind me, "I told you I could do it in twenty minutes. Leave the key in the ignition."

"OK—but I want you to know the reason why the sticker is expired—my son died unexpectedly"—and then, because he is just staring at me, I add— "He killed himself nine months ago."

He stares at me for about three seconds and then asks, "Is the battery dead?"

I pretend this is a totally normal response, so I quickly respond, "Oh, no, my husband and I have driven it around the block many times"—which is a lie because we have driven it many times on country roads, as it is perfect for muddy, snowy, potholed parking lots for trails that we walk during the cold, somber winter. When we notice that the sticker had expired months ago—oh well. Details like this, once VERY significant, are just that—details. We say to each other, let's get it done, sometime soon.

So today, oddly, an "anniversary" of his departure from this planet, is the day. I go for a twenty-minute walk while the car gets inspected, crying to myself, not just because the guy is a jerk, but because *I am the one* who shared my painful reality with a stranger who deflected it so easily. I have had this cold-shoulder response before: the woman at the fitness club stares at me when I explain the reason for changing my membership from family to individual, followed by, "Will you be using the same credit card?"

I am in a funk. I head up the street, towards the main drag, thinking I might go the library and read, and then I abruptly turn around and start walking in the other direction, a woodsy bramble of trees, bushes, vines, and a creek on my left. I am mad at the whole situation, and suddenly, at myself for *believing* that Andrew is with me. I recently returned from a three-day trip to Alexandria, Virginia, to see Michaela, and while we walked through a beautiful nature preserve, I heard Andrew singing brilliantly as a cardinal, as he so often does, high up in the trees, but I couldn't *see* him. I see him regularly in and around my hometown, not only as a regal, operatic cardinal, as a very friendly dragonfly, and a gentle young deer, so I found myself perplexed, sad, and disappointed not to see him spying on his mother and his sister as we walked for miles around the beautiful suburbs of Alexandria.

Now, as I stumble down Charles Street, feeling pissed at the world, I say out loud, "Where were you? I didn't see you in Alexandria, and I can't see you now! Maybe you are not a cardinal! Maybe I am just making *all* of this up! Maybe I am making *everything* up, and you are not with me at all!"

Then I see him. At the very moment my tirade ends, a flashy streak of bright red rises from the ground with great speed right next to me at a 45-degree angle, straight toward a medium-sized tree, like an actor making an entrance. Then, just as suddenly, the brightest cherry-red cardinal I have ever seen in my life *plops* himself down on a sturdy branch: his stage, perfectly framed by two twigs. With his body positioned like a Shakespearean actor, he looks straight at me. He is about one and a half stories above my head, and he looks right into my eyes. Then he starts to lecture me.

At this point I am well-versed in cardinal songs, but this is a stern retribution. I see his yellow beak opening and closing at a rapid rate as he reprimands me with a piercing *pyuu, pyuu, pyuu . . . pyu, pyu!* which translates in my mind as, "How can you doubt that I am here, with you, as a cardinal? You can't do that! I have shown you to myself many times, I am here right now, right here!" His puffed-out red torso and tufted head are bouncing up and down with the tremendous effort of talking to me rapidly as he continues to maintain eye contact while I can barely believe this is happening. What does one do in the midst of a bona fide miracle? I don't dare use my phone to take a picture and risk offending him, or worse, scare him away—I don't even think of it. I eventually take a quick look to my right to see some folks loading groceries into their car from the food pantry, and when I look to my left, there is no one there, so this monologue is just for me, and when I turn back to the tree with the cardinal, he is still going at it—just staring at me and scolding me for having doubts. When he finishes, he waits for me to respond. I don't know what to say, so I open my mouth and softly tell him, "I love you, Andrew." He continues to look at me, and after a short pause, with the softest chirps that a bird could make, and the volume more than half than what it was a moment ago, he replies, "I love you," or in bird speak, *pyu . . . pyu-pyu*. I say it again. He pauses, and just as softly, *he says it again*. There is nothing more to say or do now but just keep looking at each other in a soft amazement of our connection.

A truck rumbles somewhere close by and a sudden breeze picks up. He quickly looks to his right, then elegantly, as if swishing his cape, does a quick exit off stage left and disappears into the woods. I run past the creek and the brambles to catch a glimpse of him, but it is starting to get dark. I run around the block from where we were, farther down the creek, and I see a small yellow bird that I have never seen before, walking about around the water's edge. I don't know if this yellow bird is connected to Andrew, but I do know my cardinal is. He made our conversation so very nonnegotiable with a flashy entrance, determined pose, and passionate lecture delivered in birdsong that was understood by my heart. And he let me know that he loves me, too.

I walk back to the shop with a lighter step. The grizzly guy sees me, averts his eyes, and keeps on walking, disappearing behind the building. Maybe he, too, lost someone he loved. I walk into the reception area, and a decade-younger, super-friendly mechanic who performed the inspection tells me the car is "all set"—against all odds, the Honda CRV has passed inspection. He smiles with his full mouth as I write him the check, and he hands me the receipt with a "Thank you" or "Have a good day"—which always helps. It is actually a great day. I am smiling as I drive the beloved Honda back home.

SEE GRANDMA?

I walk down the short, coarse sandy beach to its end, wade into the tops of my thighs, and dive under the ropy line of small red-and-white striped buoys that separate non-swimmers from swimmers. Day campers are having lunch or playing tag or hide and seek at the moment; I enjoy the thought of a swim in relative peace.

As my head emerges from the green lake water, I immediately see Andrew the dragonfly, doing his happy, zany, figure eight-dance right in front of my face, as if to say, "Hi! I'm so glad you're here!" He settles himself onto a buoy and then just sits there—waiting for my next move. I observe him closely. He has golden, transparent wings, a gossamer fabric that a princess would covet, that let the sun shine through as he gently lifts and lowers them. He has a sleek, dark body with circles around his exoskeleton, a tail that curls upwards, and a Lego Bionicle-looking head. After I admire his coolness for five to ten minutes, I tell him I am going to do laps for a little while, thinking maybe he will still be around when I am done.

After a blend of various lazy strokes, I pop my head up and look around, feeling disoriented for a moment, and lo and behold, he is still there on the same red-and-white buoy on the rope where I left him twenty minutes ago. I stand up with my feet sinking into the mushy lake's bottom that goes up to my ankles, ignoring the gross factor for the greater good, and I talk to Andrew. I go a step further—I rest my hand on the buoy right next to his body. Your move, my son.

He takes about ten seconds to consider, and then he gingerly steps onto my index finger. And stays. I feel his tiny but strong little legs standing firm. I feel a slight vibration that tingles down into my fingers into my hand and arm. I am in "I can't believe this" mode. The day campers are back in the water splashing and racing out to the white plastic dock, but I stay put in my own little spot at the end of the designated swim area with my son in dragonfly form.

I gently tilt my hand this way and that as I marvel at this prehistoric creature until he flies off daintily to the next buoy over. I follow him and present my hand again by laying it next to his body. This time he hops onto my middle finger and sits, contentedly. I get a closer look at his face and big eyes and wings that an angel would wear for Christmas finery. He stays until he is ready to fly back to the original buoy. I walk back and present my full hand, fingers spread. He thinks about it, and then hops onto the top of my hand.

Then I pet him. I gently stroke his wings. All four of them. One at a time. The two top wings. The two bottom wings. Very, very lightly. He doesn't move, except for a small, almost nonexistent, lifting and lowering of his golden wings. *Do I dare pet his body? OK, but very gingerly. I am nervous about touching his head. I wonder if he would be OK with that. Better not be too greedy, nor risk freaking him out, since he is being so OK about my touching him. This is beyond cool. Is anyone watching? Probably not. Well, good. I'm glad no one notices. I don't want them to. This is my miracle.*

The pattern continues: he hops onto one of my fingers, on my thumb, or on the back of my hand, I pet him, then he flies off to one of three small buoys, and I follow him, and we repeat. I wonder how long we can keep doing this before he gets tired of it, and I am aware in the back of my mind that my eighty-six-year-old mother is sitting alone at the far end of the beach. She cannot walk unassisted, but I have a sudden idea on how she might be able to share this miracle with me. It is a big maybe, so the next time Andrew flies to the next buoy in our game, I tell him I'll be right back.

I dodge buckets, sandcastles, and little kids to reach my mom who is reading in the shade of a tree. I drop down onto the blanket and tell the story, then urge her to come with me so I can show her, with no idea if I can actually execute this for someone who will not be going into the water. With a cane in one hand, and her arm looped in my elbow for stability, we make our way back down the beach.

Since I left, the dragonfly has moved CLOSER, into the shallow designated swim area, on a small buoy that is about four feet from the shoreline. This makes my plan even easier! He was just waiting for my return and his grandmother, too. My goal is to bring him to her.

I walk out to the buoy. He flies one buoy away. I walk over, and he flies back to the original one, closer to his grandma and the shore. I point her out to him quietly, "See Grandma?" She can't see him from the beach; she has macular degeneration, and the sun is reflecting off the water. I am determined, however, so I walk back and hold my finger out, but he wants to keep playing. Back and forth I go, buoy to buoy, and he always reappears, ready to play some more.

He finally stops and stays still. I extend my finger. He hops on. I tell him, "I am going to bring you now to see your grandma." I walk very, very slowly, and he stays on my finger, cool and unrattled. I reach the shore, walk up the beach, and bring him right to her face. She can see him now. She looks at him and says, "Hi, Andrew" with a smile that I don't see too often, genuine delight and love. She watches him for a bit, and then she slowly lifts her index finger and rests it next to mine. He waits a moment, and then I ask him, "Do you want to see Grandma?" He walks from my finger to hers, with one big step.

Andrew and Emily had a special bond. She wrote to him, called him, and thought about him all the time. She loved taking him out to dinner and finding the best out-of-the-way spot for him to sit. She shared classical music with him, giving him cello lessons when he was a little boy. There are sweet pictures of the two of them together, her looking adoringly at him, him smiling and feeling comfortable while holding her hand or having her arm around his little body. She knew he was struggling in his later years, but she always thought about him, and was delighted when he came with me one weekend to her apartment, where he comfortably slept on the kitchen floor. That was the last time he saw her, until now.

He stays on her finger for ten seconds. And then he flies away. I am so happy that she saw her grandson Andrew, who she adored, and that he saw her, too.

TUESDAY WITH CARDINAL AND DEER

Shelby, our small orange-and-white tabby who we adopted four months after losing Andrew, is staring at something outside the window of our family room from her perch on the ledge. I hear a cardinal singing close by, loudly, so I pop up from the couch to see and hear a wild flutter of red wings next to the window. The cardinal flies from our air conditioner to the top of a weather-beaten wooden fence in our backyard. Then he looks at the house he once lived in. I race from window to window to get different views at him as he hops and moves around, sometimes looking at me, but mostly at the house. Then, he pops his head through an open part of the link fence and turns his head left and right, outside the place in the home where Andrew used to pace, back and forth, up and down a hallway.

Throughout the day, I see and hear this loud cardinal as well as his quiet mate, a pretty, yellow-red female with chunks of leaves in her mouth who dives in and out of a scraggly lily bush outside my bedroom window. While she bustles about inside the bush, shaking the leaves, I wonder, is she making a nest—in July? Are they expecting a family? This would be a healing spot for a family of cardinals to be born. The lilac bush is right near the spot where the gurney rounded the bend outside the fence to bring our beloved son to the black vehicle at the curb.

Cardinal Andrew continues to hop along the top of the fence, looking at the house and at me looking at him, then he zooms up high into the branch of a tree to sing loud and proud, in full, regal view.

Later that day, I look out the same window to see a young deer startle and jump as he becomes aware of my presence. He is near that same, tough spot, where Andrew last turned the corner of our house. He runs gently away for about five seconds, and then he turns around to look at me. Through the glass window, neither of us move a muscle for about twenty seconds as we look into each other's eye solemnly, but with a comfortable recognition. He finally turns to delicately walk his way back into the woods.

Today is Wednesday, and it is a repeat of Tuesday. Male and female cardinals are still doing their thing all day long at the corner of our house, and a family of parent deer and two fawns greet me on my lawn when I come home from the post office, stopping to look right at me first for a good long while before they prance together into the woods.

As I write here on the deck, I hear a cardinal serenading me. He is so loud, I can't concentrate, and so I try to find him, as I do every day. With the trees so full of leaves from all the rain, it is hard to spot him at first, but then I see him—standing tall, facing me, at eye level, singing his clarion song.

Then he bursts out of the tree like a rocket ship heading right toward my face and I think, *What is happening*? He's done that move as a dragonfly, but never as a cardinal! Right before he reaches my face, he angles upward, swoops over my head, and disappears from my view. Off to scan the length of the whole house and to reconnect with his little wife.

Is he comforting me? Is he reminding me that even if he didn't love the house *then,* he loves it, or is fascinated by it, now? Is he letting us know that he loves me and Jim as well as Joey (the cat he claimed to dislike), and Shelby, the cat he never met? Are his visitations daily blessings of the house that he couldn't live in while in human form, and yet seems to want to visit now?

I ask my therapist how I can distract myself from moments of great pain, and she tells me to focus on the memories. She clarifies that she is not referring to memories of Andrew in his earthly incarnation—she means the memories of the signs, his communications, and the almost daily miracles. And so, I will myself to remember the dragonfly at the lake, the cardinal in my backyard, and the deer that connects to me with those big, brown eyes. These memories are soothing.

But I still miss his body.

When Andrew is eight or nine, I visit a psychic because I am having a hard time raising him, this lively, spirited boy with the challenge of autism. She laughs and says that one day he will completely drop his ego and become my spiritual teacher. One might say her prophecy came true, but if given the choice, I would still sign up for the angry young man who lives with us while we try to figure out how we can best help him.

Now, I allow him to help me through my grief with his lively presence. By cheering me with loving and funny antics expressed through cardinal, deer, and dragonfly, and whatever other means he finds access to, he proves he is still with me in this earthly realm.

He proves to me that his life is still existing after his death.

LADYBUG

It is our shared belief that to sleep in the house on the saddest of nights is not an option, so once again, we decide on the beaches of Rhode Island. The motel room is booked, the seasonal beach pass is purchased online, umbrella and beach chairs are jammed in the back of the car, and off we go for three days and two nights.

As we drive, I think back on a memory from last year.

We are not all that familiar with the Rhode Island coastline, so we make it a goal to beach hop to get the lay of the land; this way, we will know which beaches will be in our top two or three. In between Roger Wheeler and Misquamicut, we are a little lost, so we pull off the main road to get our bearings and recheck Google maps. Once the car stops, I notice a ladybug on the top of my hand. It is just resting there on my wrist, not moving. I turn my hand slowly as it walks around the other way, so gravity won't force it to fall off. Now it has moved onto my palm and is crawling toward the base of my thumb. Jim and I sit there silently and watch it, and he snaps a few pictures. The ladybug is content to stay in this hot car with the window down on my hand, so we all just take a little rest. I think to myself, this is Andrew saying hi, just checking in, as he likes to do.

Ten minutes later, Jim is antsy about getting to the beach, but he is also very patient with bugs and insects that inhabit our lives to the point of always wanting to make sure they are safely removed (such as cupping stink bugs against the wall and bringing them outside). He sees a nice bush nearby with a peekaboo view of the ocean, and he thinks the ladybug will like it there. He opens the car door for me so I can gently walk over to the bush and encourage the ladybug to leave my hand. It takes a few moments, but we manage to safely transition the ladybug from my hand to the seaside bush. We go on our way. We enjoy the beaches, we process the grief, we get through.

Fast-forward back to the present day: July 22, 2022. We go to Scarborough Beach early on a Friday morning, and since it is a perfect blue-sky day, we patiently wait in a line that inches forward until we are *in,* feeling like we won the lottery. It is indeed a beautiful beach with soft, white sand, albeit crowded with umbrellas and everyone tanning in their chairs, so it takes a little while to find a spot that has a view of the waves—not too close for tide changes, but not too far away so we miss on out on sea breezes. The waves look amazing and scary-big for my taste.

Jim absolutely loves huge waves, and he is a master at bodysurfing. I am a novice, and for the rare times it works for me, I love it. When it doesn't work, I get pummeled. I was his apprentice last year, and I did catch some good waves where I felt the *rumble rumble* underneath my body and the top-of-the-world feeling on my face, but I don't have the innate sense for it. I purchased a bright pink boogie board last year, which helps . . . sometimes. Other times, it gets swished around my body as I flip head over heels like a rag in a washing machine and end up with my head getting pounded into the sand—take that, mere mortal! But because I want to be a trooper on this sad day, and the water feels great, I don't give up, and not unlike a surfer, there is the notion that the NEXT wave will be the best and I will ride it all the way to the shore with a big smile on my face of having nailed it!

Well, the very next wave, the ocean nails *me* with the boogie board not only strapped to my wrist but wrapped around my torso, leaving a sizable rope burn underneath my armpit, but here's the cool part: I stand up for a quick moment in between waves, and lo and behold, there is a ladybug in my hair. The ladybug is sitting on the left side of my ocean-twisted mess of tangled sandy hair, red and black and clear as day, calmly acknowledging the drama of the moment of an approaching wave, to the point when I exclaim, "What are you *doing* here?!" And just then, as if I am in one of those movies where the character gets hit and is suddenly thrust from one world to the other— like Dr. Strange getting jolted into the next multi-verse—I am slammed down again and dragged along the ocean floor until I can finally pull myself up to my feet to call out, "Jim! Jim!" to tell him about the ladybug in my hair.

When we get back to the hotel that night, I do a little internet research, and it turns out ladybugs like the ocean! It cools them off, and they can even swim in it. They are also a little bit like humans in that they can hold their breath for about the same amount of time. That bit of data confirms that I was NOT hallucinating when seeing the ladybug in my hair in between wave slams, but that once again Andrew's spirit hopped onto a nearby ocean-loving-ladybug to take a little ride in my hair for a few moments.

A week later, I am having a long phone conversation with Susie about what happened over the weekend, and I jot the word "ladybug" on a sheet of paper. About five minutes later, I look down on the sheet, still while talking to Susie, and there is a live ladybug sitting on the aforementioned white sheet of paper, next to the word! My ladybug friend is looking up at me with aviator-glasses eyes but not moving—just sitting next to the word "ladybug" itself, providing an adorable, live visual.

I don't mention this amazing fact to Susie while talking, but through it all, I am thinking to myself: *I see you, Andrew, I see you!* After finishing the call, I pick up the paper and turn it this way and that, and the ladybug steps in the opposite direction so he doesn't fall over. We enjoy each other's company for a few minutes, then he splits his domed wings in two, flies close to my face, and I quite literally have no idea where he goes next.

The synchronicity of the ladybug suddenly appearing on this piece of paper right next to his namesake makes me wonder: Is he joining the company of deer, dragonflies, and cardinals?

The next day I tell Jim. I write up and send this chapter to Susie, who loves it.

Sometimes there are so many miracles that I actually have to wait until the next day when things calm down enough to share them.

Two months later, we are in Saugerties, New York, at a pizza place, when Jim taps my shoulder. I turn around, and he says, "You have a ladybug in your hair."

Jim and I have a theory that Andrew can move in and out of the matrix, as it were, by seeing a bright bird or insect that he can pop up into to get my attention. Andrew is so connected to me in a playful way, that he can even use a ladybug to land on my hand, in my hair, and on a piece of paper I am writing on to say hello, just by jumping in.

Andrew, you are showing up for me now with ladybugs, too? Well, you have spot-on timing, kid.

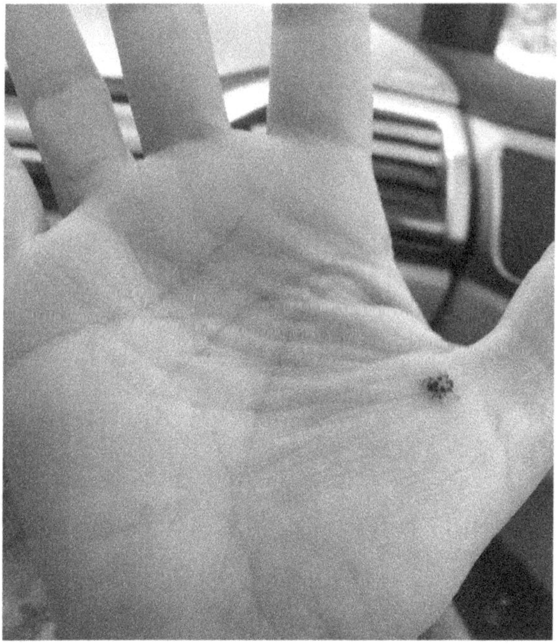

PART VI

DREAMS AND VISITATIONS

DREAMS AND VISITATIONS

The dreams and visitations are gifts from Andrew. Besides being miniature movies, Oscar-worthy indies, they are made just for me, and often just for Jim, too, who has his own dreams from Andrew—but that is his story to tell.

The dreams are poignant, bittersweet, magical, heart-breaking, and sometimes shattering in their message. Every visitation serves a purpose, such as helping me process and understand the reasons why he left us *and* allowing me the joy of seeing, hearing, and even hugging him. A visitation from Andrew involves sensory interactions: strong eye contact, extreme close-up of his facial details, a telepathic conversation where we hear each other's thoughts, and human touch passing between us. It is a big deal when I wake up and realize I just had a visitation, as I call out, "Jim! I saw Andrew!"

In many of these dreams, I chase Andrew to come back to me, safe and sound. Even though my logical self knows I cannot reach him, I must somehow still believe in my heart that I will find him, a bittersweet juxtaposition. In visitations, he often appears as a spiritual messenger who delivers lessons that I need to hear. Some lessons are sweet, others are harder to take.

Then there are visitations that allow me to experience what life is like for him on the Other Side, such as the dream of him running in hiking boots. In these dreams, he is often the age he was when he died, and I am comforted to see how at peace and how happy he is in his own realm, back to Source.

I also have dreams that are short clips that give me glimpses of Andrew as my little boy. These dreams are a healing shot in the arm as they reveal Andrew at different ages and stages in real or fantastical settings; happy, short visits that involve smiles and joy. They help heal one of the saddest parts of losing my son at age twenty-four, because I feel like I lost everything: the baby, the toddler, the grade-school kid, the middle schooler, the high schooler, the college kid, as well as the anxious young man pacing in the basement. This may not make sense—I *did* experience all his growing-up moments whereas many parents who lose children at very young ages grieve for not having those memories at all. In my case, happy memories are painful because he *is not here now*, and whatever joys he experienced as a child were not enough to sustain him in the long run. This is why I adore the visitations from Andrew where he appears to me at various ages and stages. They allow me to see him again when he is not so hurt and just pure and sweet.

I feel immense gratitude to receive a visit from Andrew when I lay my head down at night to sleep. Every time I see him is a gift.

FALLING INTO ME

Andrew is running away from me and Jim down an Old West-style boardwalk, and we can't keep up with him. He is excited about being here, and his legs are long and gangly. He is about twelve or thirteen years old, but I can only see the back of him. Just when I think we've caught up, he doubles back and starts running the opposite way. We are fast on his heels when he quickly enters a movie theater with a brightly lit marquee. We are suddenly at a fork and purposefully cut off from him; he goes into the movie theater, but we are not allowed. Instead, we drift, floating away, unmoored from gravity. I say to Jim, "I think we should meet him in the lobby," and just like that, we are all three in the lobby together. Andrew, however, leaves quickly by pushing through double doors, and once again we are following him, unable to catch up, but now on a different street.

Suddenly the dream shifts to a wide-angle shot of just me and Andrew walking side by side, about four feet apart, down a wide avenue that looks like the movie set of an old-fashioned city neighborhood. There are no other people there; it is just the two of us. The pace slows down, and Andrew starts asking questions, such as, "What is this?" I respond, "This is a street" as I point to a sign that says, "Street." We walk to the end of the boulevard and make a right into a cul-de-sac that has a very small shop at the end, and we go in. Inside, there are cooking and household supplies, pots, pans, and brooms, and Andrew immediately starts tapping and banging on the objects, listening to the sounds they make, as if he has never seen these things before. I silently watch him.

Suddenly he stops and stands quietly in a corner with his arms by his sides. I walk over to him, inches away from his face, and we make deep eye contact. He looks a bit wary as I say softly to him out loud, "It's really you, isn't it?" He looks intently into my eyes to confirm. I ask, "Can I hug you?" He bows his head and reaches out for a hug. Our arms wrap around each other's waists, and I ***feel*** *the skin on his lower back right through his shirt. After we hug, we separate a bit, he looks at me, and then he falls forward, right into me with a gentle melting motion.*

The visitation dissolves gently as I wake up.

From chasing him with Jim, to mother and son quietly walking side by side, to just the two of us in the store, the visitation evolves to us looking right at each other, a hug, and then his fall into me. This proves he is always with me, even if I forget and think he is not. Those final moments are priceless, and I think about them often.

The fact that he is fascinated with earthly things, such as the name of a "street" and solid, everyday objects, such as pots and pans, teaches me that once he left earth, he put away earthly things, and yet here he is, delighted to see them again, as if he misses them! He is in awe of Earth, as if it has been a long time since he ran down a street and felt gravity; at the same time, his old home feels like a movie set to him, and not "real." This lengthy visitation gives me a lot to think about when I consider his own process of leaving us and yet deciding time to time to return to the earthly realm from the Other Side for a visit.

The hug is pure bliss.

ASCENDING MASTER

I am standing in a suburban neighborhood, high up on a hill that descends a steep slope to a downtown area, and I am chasing my five-year-old Andrew during Halloween. I can only see the back of his head as he disappears into a crowd of kids in costumes at the bottom of the hill. I lose him, and he becomes a lost child that I don't see again until he is much older.

The dream fast-forwards to my still looking for him as a young adult, and the sense is that I have been searching for him every day since I lost him. I am now on top of a desolate, dry mountain with no one and nothing around but a rectangular, concrete, nondescript building with small windows at the top. I look down the mountain and scream at the top of my lungs, "ANDREW!" and I hear a voice that says, "I'm here." I turn around and see Andrew standing in front of a cave, as if he has emerged from it, Christlike, a seven-foot-tall young man dressed professionally in a dress shirt, belt, and khaki pants. He speaks again, "Here I am, Mom." He walks forward to hug me, and interestingly, he starts getting smaller until he is the same size as me (five feet, two inches), and we hug as equals in height and heart to heart.

I ask what he has been doing all these years that we were apart, and he points to the building. We go inside, and there is a woman who is warmly supervising an open classroom with nothing in it but a group of young boys ranging in age and of many ethnicities. Then, the walls dissolve and the boys are running around in a wide, open field. The woman asks Andrew how "Woodley" is doing in his studies, and Andrew replies that he is doing very well. I ask the woman who these boys are, and she says, "These are all my boys—Andrew is, too."

I realize that Andrew is being taken care of by this mother figure along with the boys, who he, too, watches with affectionate smiles. It strikes me that he is in a school or program with her as his teacher, and he is both a senior student and a mentor to the younger boys. When I look back at him, he is smiling and relaxed.

I wake up and wonder if this visitation is showing me that Andrew is an ascending master, content, calm, and wise, and he wants to share with me a spiritual mentor and the school for his evolvement.

Years later, in my session with the Akashic Reader, I am told Andrew is deep into his tutelage as an ascending master. I think of a psychic reading decades ago when the psychic told me that one day Andrew will be a great spiritual master. These readings give me a sweet feeling that he is learning, he is growing, he is loving others, and he is loved and cared for by those around him.

What a bittersweet thought it is.

ON STAGE

I am in the auditorium of a high school theater production that Andrew is appearing in. I am sitting next to my friend Karen, in Seattle, and I am nervous because this is a very big deal for Andrew. He will be acting in a two-person scene on stage, and it is a role with a lot of responsibility.

The play opens with a dance number that he is not a part of, but as soon as it is over, Andrew enters upstage left with his scene partner, and they begin talking to one another in character, quite naturally, as if they have known each other for years. They are both in their young twenties. They stroll while engaged in an easy-going, back-and-forth dialogue, crossing from downstage left to downstage right, and I am riveted—how easy this is for Andrew! He is not nervous or self-conscious at all as he interacts with his fellow actor, a tall, handsome Black man with a short, neat afro and 70s-style pants and shirt. What I notice is how very connected they are to one another, and although I can't hear their dialogue, it is deep to both of them. I am drawn into the scene, as is the audience.

When the scene is over, Andrew and his partner become part of the large ensemble that enters, and they all begin singing and dancing in a huge production number. I marvel at Andrew's ease with the choreography, as if he has been dancing all his life, and it is effortless. The dance number ends, and the curtain comes down for intermission, and I tell Karen I am going backstage to find Andrew and tell him what a great job he is doing in the play.

I immediately see Andrew backstage left, sitting on the ground underneath a campsite-type lean-to, dipping pita chips in hummus. He is eating quickly because he needs to go back onstage soon. I stand above him and say, "Andrew, you are doing such a great job! I am so proud!" He doesn't answer or even look at me, but I get it: he is hyper-focused on eating his snack and he needs to get refueled before Act II. I go on to ask him, "Who is your partner on stage? You two have such good chemistry," but he still doesn't respond. I interpret this to mean he is in the zone—he is so focused on staying in character that he can't let me into his head, but I am not insulted; I am proud of his focus. I tell him, "Have a great rest of the show!" and I move around the corner to find other actors to congratulate; however, I can't find anyone else, and the atmosphere is completely foggy and misty.

Then I wake up, but here is the weird part: I sit up in bed and think about this enjoyable, affirming dream, and I start telling Jim, who is sleeping. Jim mumbles "uh-huh" and does not wake up, so I lie down and instantly fall back asleep. The dream continues. That has never happened to me before.

The setting is changed, and the time has shifted to the next morning, but I am still in the same storyline. I am in my family's old house in Hyde Park, New York, and I think to myself that Andrew went to the cast party and got home late, so I tiptoe past his "bedroom," so I don't wake him up. While I am in the hallway, however, I hear his voice talking to my family, and as I enter the kitchen, there he is, sitting at the table having breakfast. I once again ask, "Andrew, who was that actor you were with on stage? He was so good, and you two had great chemistry!" Andrew casually responds, "Oh, yeah, his mom is Tina Turner." I say, "Really? That is so cool!" He laughs a bit, and says, "Yeah, he lives around here." I am astonished as I respond, "He does?" Andrew smiles and eats more of his breakfast.

Then I wake up.

The first thing I do is look up on my phone any information about Tina Turner's children. I find out that her first-born son, Raymond Craig Turner, died of suicide on July 3, 2018, at the age of fifty-nine. He was a successful Realtor in Los Angeles, not married, and very close to his mother.

Andrew died on July 23, 2020, two years and twenty days later. I burst into tears. I do not know anything about Tina Turner's family or children. I am stunned. I think about the synchronicity of souls' lives and how the spirits of Andrew and Raymond are connected on the Other Side. The pictures I see of Raymond as a young man look just like the handsome actor I saw walking on the stage in my dream. My heart experiences the same pain that Tina Turner felt. My intention always was to reach out to Ms. Turner about this dream, but now she, too, is on the Other Side with both of her sons.

I love this dream. Andrew is singing, dancing, and acting his heart out, talents and skills he would have loved to continue if mental illness had not been a part of his trajectory. I love the idea that he has a community of spirit friends, such as Raymond Craig Turner.

CAMEOS

In reading certain books about visitations from the Other Side, I learn that the spirit self has different ways, or strategies, of accessing the dream world. Andrew sometimes appears as the central focus of a dream from beginning to end, or he can slip in at a crucial middle spot and the dream suddenly *becomes* about him. Additionally, he makes cameo appearances in what I experience as short dreams. These short visits are vivid, and they deliver a message of joy while showing me his full face and body at different ages and stages. I treasure each one, no matter how brief. Here are a few cameo dreams:

Andrew is young, about seven, and with his sister Michaela, about to set out on adventures in Paris. She slings an arm across his shoulders as he swings his around her waist. He turns around and flashes me his beautiful face and a big smile, and they continue on their way.

Andrew suddenly notices he does not have the challenge of autism, depression, or anxiety anymore. He swirls around, dances, jumps, and smiles at me as a happy-go-lucky teenager, and communicates telepathically: "Look, mom, this is me! This is what I would have been like!" There is pure joy in my heart during the dream, and sadness when I wake up.

I see Andrew on a skateboard, a breezy older teenager, snaking through a crowd with a line of peers skating behind him. He is the leader! He is the cool kid, something he always wanted to be. In this realm, all his former challenges have fallen away, and I see how much he is enjoying being the guy that everyone admires.

I hear the sound first—it's a piano pounding: BOOM. BOOM. BOOM. I walk into a historic, richly decorated Spanish villa with an archway into another room where I see Andrew sitting at a piano, his arms rising high before pounding down onto the keys, hitting the same chord over and over. It is a powerful message of being seen and heard.

I am elated when Andrew expresses himself in multiple, miraculous ways to me. He struggles so much on Earth, on this confounding planet, but in these dreams, he shares with me the magnificent and limitless Spirit he is.

PART VII

THE PATH FORWARD

BACK TO KRIPALU

When Kripalu, my favorite yoga center, nestled in the Berkshires, closes for a year due to COVID, I feel the interruption keenly, sadly imagining empty halls devoid of the happy chatter of purposeful yogis walking from class to workshop to dining hall. I imagine what will happen when it reopens. When it finally does, I realize I need to attend a day of Retreat and Renewal as soon as I can make it work. My husband and therapist agree this is a great idea for my mental health.

I head west on the Mass Pike by myself, tense, angry, filled with stress. I cry and scream and curse at myself in the car. I am not doing well. I need this more than I need anything at this moment.

That cold April morning, after a 6:30 a.m. yoga class and a warm, delicious, silent breakfast, I feel my soul exhale. I empty myself out. I let go of *me*, that part that has been cynical and burned-out. *Now I am here,* feeling at home and at peace, reaching and stretching into yoga poses, rolling on the floor and swirling with scarves in a playful, movement workshop, and enjoying my meals with a view of the lake and the mountains through the window.

I am familiar with the calming indoor spaces of Kripalu, but for the first time, I do something new—I walk out the back doors and spend a slightly rainy, muddy time in Kripalu's outside spaces with no agenda but to wander and explore. Immediately, I connect to a powerfully calming source of energy. I accept the quiet, open invitation to walk and discover places I have never seen, such as Swami Kripalu's garden at the top of a flight of stairs in the woods. I slip down fairy-tale trails that follow the singing of rushing brooks, I cross tiny wooden bridges, and I walk the pine tree labyrinth while repeating the mantra, *I. Love. You.* to myself with every single step. All of it allows me to drop the negativity in my head and reconnect to a version of me that I used to know—or maybe this is a newly minted me, who wakes at 5:30 a.m. to be on the mat by 6:30, takes three yoga classes in one day, and stays through the final workshop that ends at 8:30 on a Sunday night. I do it all with a full smile on my face and a quiet sense of peace in my heart that has been long absent.

I head home with a handful of papers and drawings from my workshops, looking forward to learning and growing even more with my next visit. When I return in May, it is with warmer winds and less clothing. I follow my routines, browsing the gift store and always buying a few treasures for myself: a Kripalu tank top, books on grief and self-compassion, gratitude and personal discovery journals, and a gorgeously illustrated deck of Goddess Tarot cards, inspired by the tarot workshop. After every session, I head straight out the front doors to plop down in an Adirondack chair facing the iconic view of the lake and the mountains while the sun bakes my face and body. Strolling across the lawn, I spot a swinging bench from a tree, and I lie down in it and give the ground a good push with my foot, swinging back and forth, back and forth, feeling fully supported.

I leave behind a tiny stone or crystal at the statues of Ganesh, Quan Yin, and the little angel at the center of the labyrinth, all in memory of Andrew. He came with me once to Kripalu, a summer long ago. I have a sweet image of him in a Tai Chi class, up on a hillside, at the back of the group in his own space, gently engaging in slow, mindful movements.

Back in my own yoga studio space at home, my practice comes alive again with prop upgrades. I roll out a new thick mat in dark ocean blue, two sturdy gray blocks, a bulky blanket, and a firm but velvet-soft bolster, all to support the newness of falling back in love again with yoga.

From the wisdom and insights I gain from retreats to recharge my spirit, I cherish it all as I deepen the yoga side of me. I keep my promise to make monthly visits to Kripalu for a year, to be warmed and comforted by all the familiar sights while exploring all that is new in a wonderful, welcoming place that invites me to be myself, whoever I am, moment to moment.

FATIMA SHRINE

I stop at the Fatima Shrine in my town, an outdoor sanctuary that honors Mother Mary on a beautiful piece of land that includes tall trees, marble statues, memorials for loved ones, inscribed benches, and the largest-ever rosary walk. And I wonder: Can this be an outdoor space for me where I can connect to Andrew? I am not sure whether it will work or not, but I will find out. I am not Catholic, and I don't label myself as a Christian; however, I feel connected with Jesus and Mary as two of my many spiritual guides that I seek refuge in, and there are statues of Jesus, Mary, and angels in this place to comfort me.

Several years ago, when Michaela and I visit Sedona, Arizona, she mentions there is an outdoor Buddhist outdoor shrine five minutes from our hotel. We check it out and love it so much that we visit the Amitabha Stupa and Peace Park three times. The Buddhist culture, iconography, and imagery is calming to me with its serene, meditating Buddhas large and small, tattered, colorful Tibetan prayer flags flapping in the wind, all with the gorgeous red rocks as the backdrop. I love visiting a shrine—it works for me in all kinds of ways, outdoors, and indoors, and it serves as a sacred portal for whomever visits.

Today it is warm and breezy and beautiful—just the right kind of day to give Fatima Shrine a try. As I walk on a path lined with great boulders, each one bearing a translation of Ave Maria, I hear the cardinal song that I know so well. And then I lift my head up from the path—and there he is—my beautiful cardinal! All of him! His beautiful red body, proud head, and full wings, all on display for me to admire in a tree directly in front of me! He looks at me, hops to a closer branch with wings aflutter, sings a bit, then flutters back to his original branch. So regal, so gorgeous, so satisfying to my soul. I am bummed that I deliberately left my phone in the car, so I take a picture of Andrew the Cardinal with my heart's camera.

When the cardinal buries himself further into the tree, I leave him be and walk down the other side of the rosary path to a monument that is an open book in stone, one page with words written about the Virgin Mary and the other side honoring Jesus. A beautiful dragonfly alights on the Virgin Mary corner of the page and watches me as I stand before the monument. I reach out to touch his wings, but he flies a bit farther away and lands again, still looking at me, but not wanting to be petted today. That's OK. I read the pages, and they are about mother and son, Mary and Jesus. Jean and Andrew. I move on and sit on a marble bench overlooking a sunken, shallow pond that has its own swarm of dragonflies, dancing together in twos and threes.

This will work.

The second time I stop at Fatima, I wander over to a small, man-made cave where several battery-lit candles are snuggled in, honoring a family group. Nearby are some tall grasses, and clinging to one blade is a dragonfly. I take a seat in front of him, and I am content to sit there as a stiff breeze blows him back and forth, as he steadfastly clings on, looking at me. After about ten minutes, he flies right toward me and lands on my head. I feel tiny feet tickling through my hair, and I say out loud, "You're on my head, aren't you?" He flies back to the same blade of grass and continues to sway. After five minutes, I reach out to touch him, and he zooms away, out of sight.

During my third visit to Fatima, I return with Michaela and Jim as my fellow pilgrims. Michaela has a new, actual camera that takes gorgeous pictures of wildlife and nature, and as we mosey along the path, I show her the spot where I sat and where the dragonfly was. And, yes, there he is now, in the same spot of tall grasses as before! I reach my hand out, slowly, slowly, and he just steps into my hand. I tell Michaela to start filming, but she already is. I call out to Jim, who has wandered away and is missing this moment, in a whisper-shout, and Michaela says, "Don't worry, I'm documenting it." She takes several pictures as the little, light dragonfly steadfastly sits in my palm, not going anywhere. Jim finally returns and sees. He doesn't speak, just watches.

The third time, I go to Fatima by myself and stop by my favorite statue of an angel because he reminds me of Andrew. The sculpted face is beautiful and smooth with closed eyes, a perfectly shaped nose, cherubic lips, oval face, and softly Grecian profile. He has full-length wings and is holding a sacrament in a cup. I look at him from all angles, absorbing his calm energy. Lately, I have been giving him a full-body hug.

I walk away and see a bench with two red painted cardinals and lightly touch the image of my favorite bird. As I do, I notice a red dragonfly on the ground, right near my green sneakered foot. I squat down slowly, slowly, and sit cross-legged right next to him. He hops on my foot. I reach out my hand next to my shoe and he delicately steps right on my hand while looking up at me. I see his cute white eyes and splayed feet. We sit companionably with the sun on our faces. I manage to take out my phone and with my left hand take a few pictures. This is love.

All through the fall, the groundskeepers put up Christmas decorations, and every time I return to Fatima, more is added. This shrine is known for its extensive Christmas lighting display, as well as craft fairs and large group gatherings with live music on the weekends, as Jim and I realize when we stop by on a Saturday. Most of the time it is a quiet place where men and women walk silently, their heads full of thoughts of loved ones, or perhaps a place where they can escape from the world as we know it for a little bit. It is a place that visitors enjoy for many reasons, and I come as a pilgrim to this purposefully serene place in nature to connect to my son through our connection.

There is a covered, open altar with a beautifully colored stained-glass Mary. I purchase a candle for five dollars and place it on a shelf. Over time, I light candles for Andrew, my mother-in-law Betty, my father who died of Alzheimer's four years ago, and most recently, for myself. The Virgin Mary in braids looks on with mercy and love as the sun streams through the window.

CHANGES

It is a week before Thanksgiving, 2019, during a freezing cold snap, when Andrew, Jim, and I move into our sprawling '60s-style ranch on a cul-de-sac. After two years in a small but expensive home in Medford, an urban community where at many times throughout the day one can hear sirens in the not-too-far distance, we hope that living in a home that backs right up into dense woods with wildlife will be calming for Andrew. But his autism, depression, and anxiety think otherwise.

On the worst morning of our lives, Jim rocks back and forth, crying that he can't keep living in this house, that it will be too hard. We pass the two-year milestone of his death. And it has been oh so very hard. But we are still here.

I remember going into Andrew's room with the lava lamp heating up to play the Bionicle board game with him. Wait, am I supposed to clear all his things out until this room is empty? *NO.* Despite the general advice to grieving parents to clear the space so your child's spirit can be free of earthly belongings, or so you don't make a shrine of their life, still,

NO. I don't *want* to sort through or give away his synthesizer, violin, his massive collection of Legos, the Bionicle's game, the lava lamp. *Definitely not* his collection of retro band T-shirts that are so worn, so soft, and still contain his smell. Jim goes into his bedroom to bury his face into those T-shirts—the red Led Zeppelin, the black Bob Marley, the threadbare, iconic David Bowie image with aviators and cigarette.

Fast-forward, two years later: Michaela has the violin and the Bowie shirt. All the other epic rock T-shirts are upstairs in a bureau drawer. I pack up his jeans and athletic pants and send them to a reservation in South Dakota; Andrew loves and respects Native American culture, and this is the least I can do. Oddly, it is very hard for me to throw away his boxer shorts—to think of doing so is a harsh reminder that he does not need them where he is, now—so I send them to an online store that recycles underwear. Changes that involve reusing or recycling makes sense in my brain, and in my heart.

Changes come slowly.

At first Jim says we can't keep the brown recliner. This is where Andrew slept, read books, and had all his Zoom calls. Jim turns it upside down in Andrew's room, which makes it worse. I suggest we bring it upstairs, and it surprisingly fits in well with our woodsy theme. The brown recliner is now prominent in our living room, and it also contains Coco, Andrew's Build-A-Bear dog. Sometimes I sit in the chair, and it is very comfortable—I can see why he chose it and loved it. A few areas still contain his smell if I inhale very deeply, but sadly, those are fading.

One day, impulsively, about three months after he is gone, I paint over the dingy-white walls in the entire basement area to a soft baby-blue sky. I select the color, buy the supplies, change into paint clothes the second I get home from work, and go to town like an amateur house painter possessed, not caring about the big drips that fall onto the brownish-green industrial-looking carpeting, which we plan to rip up anyway.

When I ask Andrew about ripping up the carpet in the basement and perhaps putting in a little kitchen for him, he replies, "No! Don't waste your money!" At the time, I think he just wants us to be frugal, but those words haunt me as I consider the real reason; it is the same reason for rejecting the brand-new Oral-B I bought him, which I find unopened, never used. It is the same reason he utters "NO!" and marches away from the dentist when she suggests surgery around a certain tooth. He doesn't want *any* changes. He doesn't *need* any changes.

I am happy when we finally rip up the carpet and now have a soothing luxury vinyl tile that looks like pale driftwood. The idea is to start working out in the basement, spending more intentional time down there, whereas we used to run down, do laundry, and run back up. Nowadays, I light a candle, crank the tunes, and row on the rowing machine for thirty minutes while the cats snoop around. We have not gotten close to his bedroom yet. But we intend to, someday.

Any changes in our home take place slowly, one step at time, in the place where Andrew lived in for only eight months. I hope someday Jim and I can actually sit down, open up the boxes, look through photo albums, and watch all the home movies. Starting off into Year Three, we still have not organized his room. Grief is exhausting, and much rest is needed in between any changes at all.

For now, and probably for a while to come, changes will continue to happen, one small paint stroke at a time.

SLOW AND STEADY

Shelby wakes me up at 6:50 a.m., crying and scratching the blinds, making it impossible to sleep any further. I love this kitty, but in the summer, I also love to sleep in. She wants me to get up and play with her, but I just can't. I beg her to come to bed and cuddle with me—she is a great cuddler when she is in the mood, kneading all the sore spots on my chest before circling around and smooshing herself in for a nap between my chin and my heart. But this morning, she will not cuddle; instead, she utters her high-pitched "No!" I have no choice but to crawl out of my messy, crumpled sheets and drag myself into the living room, where I lie on the lumpy purple velour couch with a pillow under my head and a light fleece blanket thrown over my body.

Luckily, this change in venue works for her and buys me more time. She jumps up and starts to knead my legs, which feels wonderful because my legs are sore. She works hard: moving her paws in a rhythmic motion up and down over my tummy, and then finally, massage done, plopping herself down low on my abdomen. This is heaven. We both drift off.

Around 8:45 a.m., I rouse from sleep, feeling more rested but not fully awake yet. Shelby is still sleeping on my stomach, and I am swimming up to consciousness when I see Andrew's calm but interested face, looking to be around age twenty. He has swept-over blond bangs, he is wearing a T-shirt and long basketball shorts, and he is sitting in a school-style desk and chair. He looks at me on the couch and asks, directly and clearly, "What stories are you working on?"

I am alert as I tell him immediately, '"The Tortoise and the Hare' and 'The Emperor's New Clothes."' He nods and smiles at me, approving this answer, and as I start to sit fully up, he gives me a kind look, then disappears.

I sit all the way up. Wow. That just happened.

What does this mean?

I think about the moral of "The Tortoise and the Hare"— slow and steady wins the race— and I know right then and there that Andrew is giving me advice. I recently left my career as an English teacher to pursue writing full time, and I am not that patient with the process. Andrew's question and approval of my answer are an affirmation that I need to stick it out, take it slow and steady, write every day, work on and finish my book, however long it takes.

For "The Emperor's New Clothes," I am more perplexed. I know the folk tale where tricksters pose as tailors who create the most amazing "clothes" for the emperor, but it is a sham—the "clothes" are invisible. Rather than admit he can't see them, the king hires the tailors to make him a royal wardrobe, and he parades himself naked down the street. I am not sure how the story applies to me in the moment, so

I quickly look it up on my phone. The moral of the story is to be true to oneself, to be honest. This is a message from Andrew that I need to hold fast to what I want to do with my life, and for the rest of my time on this earth. This means writing honestly and openly about what is happening to me.

It is almost three years after he left, and I just received Andrew's words of wisdom in a morning visitation! He comes to remind me of what is important to me as a writer, and as a person. As the impatient, wandering soul that I am, I will continue on, Andrew, slow and steady, honoring the truth of my experiences.

STILL GRIEVING, YEAR THREE

I wish I could say that grieving during Year Three is a lot easier than Year One and Year Two. My grief is with me all the time, but it is a *tiny* bit easier. The panic attacks of my heart have eased in frequency, but when they hit, they hit hard and long. They also occur more unexpectedly, such as a pain that rises and clamps my heart right in the middle of mosaics class so that I must leave everything behind, race to the car for the five-minute drive home, and dive under the covers for twenty-four hours with my clothes still on.

I cry hard when I am sad—it's like I need to let it all out for a while, and then I can get on with my day—or I just call it a day, depending on how sad I am. When certain songs come up, I sometimes actually go ahead and listen to them to celebrate Andrew OR I skip ahead to a track that has no connection to Andrew, or to loss. It depends on my inner strength. I have a dull resignation that comes up time to time to remind me that this really sucks. After exploring it from many angles, I still can't fully comprehend why he is not here, in our house, peeking around the corner to see if we are in a certain room. I will take him back! Just as he is! But the house is silent and still.

I still don't believe that time heals. I lost my child, my son, my little boy, and time alone *cannot heal* this fact. Furthermore, the more time passes, the more the chasm of time increases between his being here with versus his not being here. I don't want his life to feel like a faraway dream. I hope this book expresses how much I want his life to be honored in the present moment, and not as a life lived long ago.

But there seems to be a path forward. Because my human soul can heal. Not completely, but I will take what I can get.

I continue to have good days, OK days, not-OK days, really bad days, but not so many really bad weeks. Time will continue doing what it does to me, so I have to do what *I* can to heal myself, and this results in my having more good days than bad. I aim to get outside once a day for a walk or bike ride, although I don't always manage it. I strive to work out at the gym once or twice a week and use the rowing machine in the basement, even if it means I cry while I row. I intend to meditate ten minutes every morning and listen to a guided meditation before bed, but I have lapses. I practice yoga with an online teacher once or twice a week, and my next goal is to visit Kripalu for a two-day workshop, not just a one-day visit, which is not enough.

Because I no longer wake up at 5:00 a.m. to teach, I wake up when my body wants to. I often write in the local library for a couple of hours, until I need to move again. Having structure helps, and writing is a way of calming and focusing my mind in the midst of chaos. So does working on a thousand-piece puzzle. To really wind down, I step outside of the intensity of my memories and emotions and watch escapist-style series and movies that don't rev up my nervous system or agitate my sore heart, such as rom-coms and stand-up comedy—no intense violence or explorations of death. I am careful about the books I choose to read, and if they are about the afterlife or grieving, I don't read them right before bed. It's too much.

When I really need to talk, the best thing to do, I remind myself, is to reach out to one of my small circles of friends and family who can spare the time, even if I am interrupting their day—which usually means Jim or Michaela. Having a therapist gives structured time when I can bounce around all over the place with my emotions, trying to make sense of it so I can keep moving forward.

If I can get out of my head for a moment, being grateful helps, too. I want to cultivate more gratitude for the life and the moments I have been granted, like the turtles who climb on a log, extend their heads out of their shells, and tip their heads to the sun, soaking up the warmth of the sun and the fact that we are still here, still alive.

Losing Andrew teaches me how strong my love for him truly is. Instead of wishing happiness and success for Andrew when candles are blown out on a cake, I silently say, "I love you, Andrew." I don't have to wish him anything but freedom and peace in the afterlife. In my heart and through my dreams, I know he has found these things.

I am grateful that while he is learning and growing as a spirit himself, he is still connecting with me, and I am grateful for my *own* ability to connect with him. I vow to never close off my channels. Seeing him has become a regular, commonplace occurrence, such as the time I step out of my car in the parking lot of the gym to greet a big, bold dragonfly, just pausing in the air, waiting for me. He is so happy to see me, zigzagging back and forth, circling me and my car, wishing me a good workout. I smile because it has become normal and joy-filled at the same time.

Every griever follows their own path. This is mine, and it continues to expand. I could not get through without my spiritual perspective, and I feel that truth in my soul, even though I may forget this truth now and then. Two things continue to be essential to my path forward: keeping myself open to any chance for happiness and joy, and dedicating myself to self-care. I am eating healthier overall, trying to get enough rest, and still trying to drive out west to Kripalu when the timing is right for yoga retreats. I am also taking my mosaics classes and creating beautiful art pieces of colored glass, sand, tile, rock, and shell, which nourishes my artistic side.

The anniversary of Year Three will soon be upon me, and I will cry long and hard. But at the same time, I might find comfort in what a Reiki healer at Kripalu said to me when I told her about Andrew's visitations: It's just Andrew, wanting to say hi, and you are still his mother. If this feels confusing or elusive, just embrace the mystery of it all.

THIRD ANNIVERSARY

Sitting at a red light, my head rests lightly on the steering wheel for a moment, tears streaming down both cheeks. I have laryngitis, so I cry without sound. I lift my head and scratchily whisper to Jim that my throat is so dry that I need moisture in the form of something cold and creamy; slugging cold water from my Hydro Flask is not cutting it. To my surprise, he states, "This is an emergency," and he tells me to make a right off the main road to look for a convenience store. I shift into the turn lane, make a right, and soon spot a Cumberland Farms where we can survey options.

This is the third year Jim and I are making the trek to Narragansett, Rhode Island, to grieve, honor, and have time and freedom to process the reality that our son Andrew died from suicide at age twenty-four on this day three years ago. About ten minutes into the drive, Jim says, "Let's get right to it, shall we?" I can't remember exactly what we talk about, but we compare good times with the very bad times, and then we get silent and depressed. I park, and we walk into the air-conditioned mart where I immediately point out yogurts nestled in a wall freezer, but he says, “Nah, let’s look at the ice cream choices.” We continue to a little waist-high freezer of chocolate-covered vanilla ice-creams on a stick, and I am content with that, but then he spots what will really do the trick—Ben and Jerry’s Americone Dream.

I grab two white plastic spoons on the way out, and as soon as we get into the car, with him driving now, he peels off the circular cardboard lid, hands the carton to me to dig in, and then takes it back without a word to dive in his spoon with his eyes on the road. For a few silent moments, we have nothing on our minds but the creamy vanilla and caramel softness swirling in our mouths interrupted by delicious pieces of fudgy waffle cones. The pint goes back and forth, our spoons moving quickly, sharing, never hoarding, experiencing this moment of therapy on equal terms.

By the time we get to the small, family-owned, ocean-themed motel right across from Scarborough Beach, there is less than a quarter left. I’ve never polished off that much Ben and Jerry’s alone or with another person in one sitting, especially before lunch, and it feels deliciously decadent and just what the doctor ordered. I walk into the cheery, white motel room, head straight to the back where a small fridge sits and pop the bit of ice cream left in the pint into the tiny freezer compartment to be finished by one or both of us later.

Time to see the ocean.

DRAGONFLY SEASON

It is Mother's Day, 2024. It has been a rough, sad, lonely winter into spring, and today is no different. Halfway into Year Three, I realize that on July 23, it will be four years since Andrew is gone. Four is a tough number to process. In four years, I graduated from high school, likewise for college. Four is the number of our family members: Jean, Jim, Michaela, and Andrew. We have four seasons, the Four Seasons hotels, Frankie Valli and The Four Seasons, four Beatles; all good things seemingly come in fours, and that makes it hard for me to accept that it has been four years since Andrew left our home. Knowing this expanse of time will only continue to increase is unbearable—especially the thought of it going beyond twenty-four years.

We are bundled up for a walk, just the two of us. There was a time when Mother's Day was celebrated with scones, fruit salad, a latte in the morning, the gift of a yellow dress from Jim, and hand-drawn cards and hugs from both kids. Celebrating Mother's Day now feels like a dated tradition that existed once upon a time.

Near the end of our walk on a path bordering a grassy meadow, I spot a large dragonfly helicoptering ahead of us, and I point out his silhouette against the light gray sky. This is the first dragonfly I have seen this season. A smile comes to my mouth, and my numb heart gets a little lift as my eyes follow him to where he lands. We reach the spot where he rests, clutching a long blade of grass with his tiny arms, his body and head facing us. As we take a seat on the dusty path, he looks at us. There is no question in our minds that this is Andrew, dropping by to say hi and stay awhile.

A slight wind pushes him side to side as he continues to clutch and cling, bobbing. We sit for ten minutes, take some pictures. And then it's time for me to touch him.

I stretch my index finger gently on his tissue-paper-thin right wing, and gently glide my finger on the back side of it. He doesn't mind at all, so I continue, tracing his upper and lower wings, his back body, and finally, his rounded, solid little head. And then something miraculous and joyful occurs: In response to my touch, he moves his tiny arms and legs, very deliberately and artistically, each one independent of the other. His movements are smooth and articulated as he engages in a hypnotic dance with arms and legs reaching, curling, extending, contracting, folding, opening, a continuous choreography of mudras. The more I pet him, the more his little antennae-sized extremities move up and down and out to his sides. Once again, I am witnessing a bona fide miracle, and all I can do is watch, embrace, and laugh at his sweet, silly, playful dragonfly spirit.

We continue our dance for ten minutes, and then I wonder, as I sometimes do, if I should not overdo it; to leave him be, to just be grateful he has come all this way in time and space to drop into this dragonfly's body to entertain me on Mother's Day. We slowly stand up and walk away while he continues to clutch his blade of grass.

As I walk toward the busy road, I take one last look behind me—he is still there. And I believe he remains there as we cross the street and into the muddy parking lot and climb into Jim's car, all in a state of wonderment.

Dragonfly season has begun! I have approximately six months ahead to visit with friendly dragonflies of all sizes and colors, dashing by my face, hovering above my head, gently landing on my outstretched palm or on a sneakered shoe. I think back on all my dragonfly experiences, and four months later, I find it the most natural thing in the world when I am at Walden Pond with my sister Becky and a big, black dragonfly deliberately plants himself on my opened palm.

A great Mother's Day gift—a dragonfly dance and kickoff to the season.

YEAR FOUR: THE PATH FORWARD

Jim and I take our walk to the lake and point out two or three intrepid dragonflies moving low near the water's edge or up high by the treetops. It is late October, and the abundant dragonfly season of late spring and summer is now drawing to a close. The yellow and red leaves are stunning this year, and I breathe in this warm stretch of blue-sky days and sun, knowing that cold and dark nights are well upon us. I wear sweatpants and flannel shirts on weekends instead of shorts and flip-flops, and before I know it, the Christmas season will be here. That's OK. The colors and the lights of Christmas lift my spirit and soften the edges of my heart. Quietly decorating the tree that faces Andrew's cabinet of mementos with my very loved collection of carefully selected ornaments—deer, cardinals, dragonflies, angels, a gold Buddha, a glass bell with Tinkerbell that miraculously made it back from a trip to Disney World, and Charlie Brown characters—brings me peace as I carry on the family tradition.

My body is physically aware of the aging process that has been accelerated by grief. When I look in the mirror, I can't help but notice the deep, downward wrinkles at the corners of my mouth, an etched-in sadness that is my face now. My quickly graying hair is covered up with frequent visits to the hair salon, and this past year, I have so many more surgeries (squamous skin cancer on my leg, grafting for my receding gums), appointments, and ultrasounds.

And yet, I think some kind of emotional healing is taking place. Year Four starts out rocky with uneasiness, anxiety, depression, and big meltdowns. But I can say this much: *I accept* that Andrew is gone and that he left because he had to. He was in so much pain, and I get it: I, too, have been going through my own version of life's heartbreak. But now I am living side by side with it and know that I always will.

Working regularly with a therapist and psychiatrist gives me the tools and the balance I need, not just to survive, but to embrace who I am, with all my flaws and inner reserves of strength. Instead of being pulled into my darkest thoughts, I accept that Andrew's leaving us is embedded in the story of my life, his life, and our family's life. We had hard times, but we had many good times, too. I am so thankful and glad that we took our kids on so many vacations, to London, Paris, the Caribbean, and Hawaii, with sunny skies and smiles in every photo. I'm glad Andrew went mountain biking in Utah with his dad and Uncle Gene. I'm glad I followed through with my idea of going to California for Christmas break one year so everyone could see where I grew up in Torrance, minutes away from Redondo Beach. On Christmas Eve, we went to

Disneyland, which was our last vacation together as a family of four. The picture of Andrew standing on a large rock on a beach at Malibu is invaluable.

Dear Andrew, I know you want me to be happy, so I will continue to hold space for laughter and joy on my path forward. I sing and dance with my sisters while my brother plays Billy Joel and Elton John classics on a piano. I cozy up next to Jim on the couch and eat dinner while we laugh at our favorite late-night comics on YouTube as a reward for getting through an exhausting day. When I jump into bed, I dutifully put on my sleep apnea mask, snuggle up to the warm kitty on my chest, and blissfully sink into a restful sleep, always hoping for some spiritually healing dreams.

I am so grateful how you always know when I really need to see you! Last week you visited me in a short dream where I saw you standing in the entrance to the kitchen wearing aviator glasses, but these were not your sunglasses. You have always had perfect vision, and you look at me now through clear lenses, symbolizing you see things so clearly, and I read the message in your face: Mom, I got you. I got your back. It will be OK.

Thank you, Andrew, for coming to earth to be my baby and letting me be your mom for twenty-four years. I can still imagine the feel of your warm, curled-up body when I was pregnant with you, so honored to be having a second child, a boy for our family and a brother for our daughter. I can conjure images of your blond toddler self, playing happily on the floor with your toys, or as an older kid, lying on your tummy and drawing Yu-Gi-Oh figures in your sketchbook. I honor your love of music, your grit, and your wisdom. I will always remember everything about you, and I will strive to live by your words of wisdom: *Don't look down. Hold your head up. Slow and steady wins the race. Be true to yourself.* You encourage me to keep moving forward. If I hold my head up, I see the warm, soulful eyes of a deer, dragonflies alighting on my hand, cardinals shining brilliantly and singing in the trees, all looking back at me with infinite, profound, caring love. You will always be my beautiful son, dear Andrew, and I will always be your mother.

ACKNOWLEDGMENTS

To Michaela for helping and supporting me with this project: I love you, dear daughter. To Avery Naughton, thank you for your detailed editorial comments, and to Asya Blue, thank you for taking on the work of designing this very important book. A big thank you to old friends, new friends, neighbors, and family members who read my first draft and provided invaluable feedback. Sending my love out to my Oregon and Seattle friends, and to my hometowns of Torrance, California, and Hyde Park, New York, for shaping who I am today. Deep love to my mother Emily Robison for her constant support of me, Andrew, and this book, and gratitude to my father Ed Robison for being Andrew and Michaela's Grandpa Donald. To David, Julie, and Becky, thank you for being Robison siblings with me, and for loving our Andrew. To my beautiful children, Michaela and Andrew, I cherish you for the unique and wonderful individuals that you are. To my husband Jim, thank you for parenting with me, for always being by my side, for being my best friend, and for the love we share.

We are always a family of four.

All photos by Jean and Jim except the cardinal in the tree on page 134, which was taken by Michaela, and the deer on our doorstep on page 126, which was taken by Pat Woods.

ABOUT THE AUTHOR

Jean Robison—Starting a career path with a BA in Dance, Jean performed in musical theater productions around the country and worked as a director, choreographer, and teacher of dance and drama. In addition to a lifelong passion for creative writing, Jean earned a MEd in English and taught English Language Arts for fifteen years in middle and high schools. She enjoys being in nature, traveling, practicing yoga, and creating mosaics. Her article, "Walking the Path of Grief," appears in the magazine, *We Need Not Walk Alone*. She lives in Massachusetts with her husband and two cats. *Deer, Dragonfly, and Cardinal* is her first book.

https://jean-robison-creative-writer.squarespace.com

www.ingramcontent.com/pod-product-compliance
Lightning Source LLC
Chambersburg PA
CBHW022201030225
21379CB00008B/261
9798992181708